THE CHRISTIAN MESSAGE FOR CONTEMPORARY MAN

STEPHEN F. OLFORD

WORD BOOKS, PUBLISHER
WACO, TEXAS

Copyright © 1972 by Word (U.K.) Ltd,

All rights reserved.

No part of this book may be
reproduced in any form, except
for brief quotations in reviews
without the written permission
of the publishers.

ISBN 0 85009 046 6

First American edition, June 1974

Printed in the United States of America

Dedicated to
A. Lindsay Glegg
whose godly life, enduring friendship and
experience in evangelism have encouraged
me, more than I can ever say, to be a
communicator of the Christian message
to contemporary man.

CONTENTS

	Foreword	7
	Preface	9
	Acknowledgments	13
1.	The Contradiction of the Christian Message	15
2.	The Character of the Christian Message	35
3.	The Community of the Christian Message	57
4.	The Communication of the Christian Message	77
5.	The Comprehension of the Christian Message	95

FOREWORD

Despite unparalleled advances in the field of technological science, our day is plagued by a great deal of fuzzy thinking, especially in the realms of philosophy, morality and religion. Christianity has been victimized by this scourge, not only from those without, but from many within the professed church. The question, 'What is the Christian message?' would evoke a confusing cluster of replies, yet capable of being reduced to a common denominator: Do good! In a word, the effect of the Christian message is mistaken for the message itself.

'Can the Ethiopian change his skin, or the leopard his spots? then may ye also do good, that are accustomed to do evil.' In these words the prophet Jeremiah affirms that what man the sinner needs is not a law, nor an ideology, nor an ethic—valuable as these are in their place—but a Saviour who can change him within and set him in a new relation to God and his fellow man.

The Apostle Paul delineates the Christian message in bold lines, and in no place is he more bold in his definitions than in this passage which Dr. Stephen F.

FOREWORD

Olford has chosen as his text for this brief treatise. Strangely enough, the apostle finds himself facing a schismatic situation in the Corinthian church. In dealing with that situation, he does not merely reprove it, but corrects it by presenting facets of the Christian message which completely prohibit division. Only let us grasp the wonder of the message, and strife over the messenger or any other lesser consideration will be ruled out.

In this excitingly lucid exposition of I Corinthians 1:9—2:16 Dr. Olford follows the keen reasoning of the apostle Paul from step to step, showing the relevancy of the Christian message for our generation. More than ever man needs a Gospel that brings to him the wisdom and the power of God. He needs a Gospel that reaches the foolish, the feeble and the fallen, for that is as much the state of twentieth-century man as of first-century man. There is no such Gospel, save that of 'Jesus Christ, and him crucified.' This is the apostolic emphasis, and this is the sword-thrust of the author of these rich studies.

Given at Filey Bible Conference in England, these studies are published essentially as they were delivered there, so that the preaching style, warm and pointed, comes through. It is the prayer of the author, and of the writer of this Foreword, that hearts will be moved by the reading, as so many were by the hearing, of these expository messages.

J. C. Macaulay
Dean, New York School of the Bible
New York

PREFACE

In his little book *Man Alive*,[1] Michael Green quotes Lord Eccles who scolds church leaders today for the unintelligibility and irrelevance of so much theological writing. His words of criticism need to be weighed and heeded when he says, 'The laity, although better informed on almost everything else, have never been so ignorant about the ground-plan of the New Testament'; and then addressing the clergy he adds: 'This is partly your fault because you have concentrated your scholarships in fields too narrow to be widely interesting; will you now turn your attention to the gospel as a whole? to its relevance as a whole to the age in which we live?' Michael Green has taken Lord Eccles seriously and has written an excellent treatment of the resurrection of our Lord Jesus Christ, showing its contemporary relevance, challenge and power to change men's lives. What is even more important is that he has couched this central fact of our Christian faith in terms that the layman can understand.

Even before I read *Man Alive* I was burdened in a similar fashion for young Christians who find it so

[1](London: Inter-Varsity Press, 1967), Preface.

difficult to appreciate and communicate the Christian message to contemporary man, and so I set about preparing a series of messages which, in the first instance, I delivered at the Filey Holiday Crusade in September of 1972. My audience was mainly young people, and so I spoke accordingly, and, I trust, appropriately. Such was the response from these youthful listeners that I was asked to share these studies in printed form. One condition I was very hesitant to comply with was that the material be published as I preached it. This I have never done before, since it violates my literary style! However, with some deletions of irrelevant asides and redundancy of words I have agreed to release the manuscript. It is my sincere prayer that the Holy Spirit will graciously use the preaching format with its fire and challenge to bless my readers, as it did the hearers.

The outlines that introduce each chapter are included to aid ministers and Christian workers in tracing the expository treatment of the first two chapters of I Corinthians. It follows, therefore, that to derive the greatest benefit from these studies, it would be well to read and reread the verses that constitute the text.

Nearly two thousand years ago our risen Saviour said, 'Go ye into all the world, and preach the gospel to every creature.'[2] Dr. Alexander Maclaren called this 'the divine audacity of Christianity.' A study of the Commission, as it appears in other parts of the New Testament, makes it manifestly clear that the Lord Jesus meant literally all the world. He meant every country of the world, for He said, 'Ye shall receive

[2] Mark 16:15.

power, after that the Holy Ghost is come upon you: and ye shall be witnesses unto me both in Jerusalem, and in all Judea, and in Samaria, and unto the uttermost *part* of the earth.'[3] No country is to be left out, however closed to missionary penetration by the Iron or Bamboo Curtains, or anything else.

Jesus meant every culture of the world—'Go ye therefore, and teach all nations, baptizing them in the name of the Father, and of the Son, and of the Holy Ghost: teaching them to observe all things whatsoever I have commanded you: and, lo, I am with you alway, even unto the end of the world.'[4] We are living in a day of emerging nations. Never before in the history of the world has such emphasis been placed on the dignity, unity and sovereignty of individual nations. Great importance is also attached to the culture of these nations, and because of this Christianity is often rejected, since it is associated with Western culture. But notwithstanding these difficulties, the Commission is to go to every nation.

And our Master meant every creature of the world—'Go ye into all the world, and preach the gospel to every creature.' God is no respecter of persons, and therefore man, whatever his color, creed, or class, must be reached with this glorious message of full salvation.

When the Lord Jesus uttered these words the world was not as accessible to the preacher and missionary as it is today, but we have no excuse now. Some years ago the President of the Royal Geographical Society chose

[3] Acts 1:8.
[4] Matthew 28:19–20.

a startling phrase to describe the modern world. He said: 'Time and distance have now been annihilated by modern inventions and have caused *a shrinkage of the globe*.' Think of the test pilot who recently broke the record of 4,000 m.p.h. through space; and now we are told that on the drawing boards, at the present time, are planes which will carry passengers at over 2,000 m.p.h. Added to this we have radio, television and astonishing advances in literacy and available literature. Having said all this, however, we must hang our heads in shame when we realise that there are over 700 million people who have never heard the Gospel of our Lord Jesus Christ, and that every day of every year over 100,000 of these people die without hope of eternal life. How urgent and solemn, then, is our task to carry the Christian message to contemporary man! May God give us the grace to catch the vision, feel the passion, and serve the mission of our commissioning Lord.

Stephen F. Olford
Encounter Ministries, Inc.
New York

ACKNOWLEDGMENTS

I want to acknowledge with profound thankfulness the many people who have helped to make possible the preparation and presentation of these expository studies on The Christian Message for Contemporary Man, based on I Corinthians 1 and 2. I would particularly mention the number of authors I have quoted; my good friend, Dr. J.C. Macaulay, who has graciously written the Foreword; and Miss Victoria Kuhl, who has typed the manuscript. To all these and more I would extend my gratitude for being willing to be part of the 'comunicating team'!

The Contradiction of the Christian Message

I Corinthians 1:9–17

I. DIVISION PARALYSES THE FELLOWSHIP OF THE CHURCH IN ITS WITNESS TO THE WORLD (v. 10)
   1. Division in the Church Degrades the Ministry of the Word of God (v. 10)
   2. Division in the Church Disrupts the Unity of the Spirit of God (v. 10)

II. DIVISION PUBLICISES THE MEMBERSHIP OF THE CHURCH IN ITS WITNESS TO THE WORLD (v. 11)
   1. Division Adversely Publicises the Name of the Church (v. 11)
   2. Division Adversely Publicises the Fame of the Church (v. 11)

III. DIVISION POLARISES THE LEADERSHIP OF THE CHURCH IN ITS WITNESS TO THE WORLD (v. 12)
   1. Devotion to Men Rather than the Master (v. 12)
      a. There were those who said they belonged to Paul
      b. There were those who said they belonged to Apollos
      c. There were those who said they belonged to Cephas

       d. There were those who said they belonged to Christ
  2. Attention to Messengers Rather than the Message (vv. 13–17)

1

THE CONTRADICTION OF THE CHRISTIAN MESSAGE

The theme I have chosen for this series of studies is 'The Christian Message for Contemporary Man.' I have elected to deal with this subject because of the new evangelical interest which is emerging in our country and lands overseas at this present time. It is true, of course, that there are many things which still concern us and drive us to our knees; but, on the other hand, it is evident that evangelists who have been on the sidelines for some time are finding extended and exciting opportunities for crusades and other Gospel activities. Young people, particularly, are giving a significant lead with their singing, witnessing and marching for Christ! The Spirit of God has been poured out in an unusual manner on some of our churches in Britain, the U.S.A. and elsewhere. Individuals have come into a fresh experience of what it means to be anointed with the Holy Spirit and to speak and serve with power from on high.

With this in mind, I invite you to peruse carefully the first chapters of I Corinthians. For this opening message, however, let us read together I Corinthians 1: 9–17.

God is faithful, by whom ye were called unto the fellowship of his Son Jesus Christ our Lord.

Now I beseech you, brethren, by the name of our Lord Jesus Christ, that ye all speak the same thing, and that there be no divisions among you; but that ye be perfectly joined together in the same mind and in the same judgement. For it hath been declared unto me of you, my brethren, by them which are of the house of Chloe, that there are contentions among you.

Now this I say, that every one of you saith, I am of Paul; and I of Apollos; and I of Cephas; and I of Christ. Is Christ divided? was Paul crucified for you? or were ye baptised in the name of Paul?

I thank God that I baptised none of you, but Crispus and Gaius; lest any should say that I had baptised in mine own name. And I baptised also the household of Stephanas: besides, I know not whether I baptised any other. For Christ sent me not to baptise, but to preach the gospel: not with wisdom of words, lest the cross of Christ should be made of none effect.

Under our main theme, 'The Christian Message for Contemporary Man,' we shall consider in order The Contradiction of the Christian Message, The Character of the Christian Message, The Community of the Christian Message, The Communication of the Christian Message, and finally, The Comprehension of the Christian Message.

Our immediate concern, then, is The Contradiction of the Christian Message (I Corinthians 1: 9–17). To examine this portion of the New Testament is to be impressed not only with the annunciation of God's grace, but also with the evaluation of man's need. Before he deals with these cardinal doctrines, however, the apostle addresses himself to the problem that had weakened the witness of the Corinthian church and, indeed, has weakened the church of Jesus Christ at every stage of her history – the problem of *division*. Our Saviour prayed against this when He faced the death of the cross, looked on to the day of Pentecost, and anticipated the discipling of the nations. Addressing His Father He prayed: '(Make my disciples) one; as thou . . . art in me, and I in thee, that they also may be one in us: *that the world may believe* that thou hast sent me.'[1]

The apostle had the same burden on his heart when he wrote to the church at Philippi. Mark well his words: 'Only let your conversation (or manner of behaviour) be as it becometh the gospel of Christ . . . that ye stand fast in one spirit, with *one mind, striving together for the faith* of the gospel.'[2] His point is that nothing contradicts our Christian message like division in the church. How can we preach the message of reconciliation when Christians cannot forgive one another? How can we proclaim the message of peace when church members are at one another's throats? So in the verses before us Paul confronts this issue head-on. In verse 9 he starts with the affirmation that 'God is faithful, by whom (all Christians are) called unto the fellowship of his Son Jesus Christ

[1] John 17:21
[2] Philippians 1:27

our Lord,' and then, without a break, he continues, 'I beseech you, brethren, by the name of our Lord Jesus Christ, that ye all speak the same thing, and that there be no divisions among you; but that ye be perfectly joined together in the same mind and in the same judgement.' Now we cannot compare verses 9 and 10 with any measure of perceptiveness without concluding that the supreme contradiction of the Christian message is division in the church. Observe carefully how Paul supports this deduction:

First, *division paralyses the fellowship of the church in its witness to the world.* 'I beseech you, brethren, by the name of our Lord Jesus Christ, that ye all speak the same thing, and that there be no divisions among you; but that ye be perfectly joined together in the same mind and in the same judgement.' Christian fellowship, as we all know, is based on two fundamental prerequisites for a local church: first, the ministry of the Word of God, and secondly, the unity of the Spirit of God. You will remember that after the day of Pentecost the early disciples 'continued steadfastly in the apostles' *doctrine* and *fellowship.*'[3] Let us stop there for a moment and recognise that there can be no true fellowship without a doctrinal basis. When writing to the Philippians, Paul speaks of this fellowship, this koinonia, as the 'fellowship of the Spirit.'[4] So we see that it is only through the truth of God that we are brought to the reconciling death of Christ, and it is only through the Spirit of God that we are brought to the unifying life

[3] Acts 2:42
[4] 2:1

of Christ. Wonderful as all this is, nothing is more calculated to paralyse the fellowship of the church in its witness to the world than division; for division strikes at the heart of these fundamental prerequisites.

Division in the church degrades the ministry of the Word of God – 'I beseech you, brethren, by the name of our Lord Jesus Christ, that ye all speak *the same thing*.' Division paralyses the fellowship of the church because there is no unity of witness in what we say; and that was true at Corinth. The strength of any testimony is that everyone says *the same thing*. In appealing to the Corinthian church for a united front, Paul employs an expression that was used in political circles for 'mutual agreement' 'or 'perfect agreement' (note the Greek there). He was not suggesting uniformity of speech. There are many ways of saying the same thing. Styles of presentation may and do differ, but truth is unchanging and unchangeable. There is a unity of testimony which must be the result of the acceptation and declaration of the truth of God. How well history illustrates this again and again! The impact of the church of Jesus Christ has been considerable when the church has said the same thing. Lloyd George, that great politician and one-time Prime Minister of Great Britain, is reputed to have said that 'whenever there was a moral question to settle, once the bells of the church rang in unison the battle was over.' When Christians say the same thing there is unity of strength and the world outside believes. It is what our Saviour prayed for when He expressed words that we have already quoted: '(Father, make them) one; as thou . . . art in me, and I in thee, that they also may be one in us: *that the world may believe that thou hast sent me.*'⁵ So Paul strongly appeals to the Corinthians to speak the same thing.

Division in the church not only degrades the ministry of the Word of God, but disrupts the unity of the Spirit of God – 'I beseech you, brethren, by the name of our Lord Jesus Christ . . . that ye be perfectly joined together in the same mind and in the same judgement.' Now follow me closely here. There is an essential unity which nothing can ever harm or destroy. As John Stott has put it: 'Our unity in Christ is essentially as strong as the unity between the Father and the Son and the Holy Spirit.' Nothing can divide us from the love of God which is in Christ Jesus our Lord. There is a fundamental unity which nothing can change. On the other hand, there is an experimental unity which can be interrupted by division. There is a rift which can come into the personal fellowship of your church, your group, even your family, and that is what Paul is speaking about here. He is saddened by the fact that the seamless robe of unity has been torn within the Christian community. The word he selects to describe this condition is the one from which we derive our term 'schism.' He says there is a schism, a rent, in the garment. William Barclay remarks: 'The Christian church was in danger of becoming as unsightly as a torn garment.'⁶ So admonishes Paul: 'I beseech you, brethren . . . that ye be perfectly joined together in the same mind

---

[5] John 17:21
[6] *The Letters to the Corinthians* (Edinburgh: The Saint Andrew Press, 1958), p. 16.

and in the same judgement.' The phrase, 'perfectly joined together,' conveys a beautiful concept. It is used in the Gospels of 'mending nets.' It is used in the first Epistle of Paul to the Thessalonians of supplying a lack.[7] Quite clearly reparation was desperately needed in the Corinthian church; thus the apostle pleads for it in no uncertain language. He calls for a unity of mind, a harmony of judgement; only such a return to the ministry of the Word of God, only such a return to the unity of the Spirit of God, could bring about a united front and a message for the contemporary age in which Paul lived. What was true then is true today.

In 1747 there arose differences and disunity among Moravian brethren who belonged to a group of local churches whose influence and missionary effort were widespread. Count Zinzendorf, with representative elders, arranged to hold a conference at which the differing views on the subject of their controversy might be aired and discussed amicably. The leaders came – some from long distances – to the place where the conference was to be held. Arriving on the appointed day, each prepared to contest the view he supported, confident that it would receive the acceptance of the majority. In his wisdom, Zinzendorf proposed that they should spend some time in the Word and in prayer. The book chosen for study was the first Epistle of John; and for several days they examined the teaching of this letter – learning that one of its main lessons was 'love for all the brethren.' They agreed that on the first day of the week, like the

[7] 3:10

disciples in the early church, they should come together to break bread, and so be reminded that they, being many, were 'one Body.' The reading and studying of God's Word and the fellowship at the Lord's Supper had a very salutary effect on all. Indeed, the result was such that when they commenced on Monday morning to examine the matters on which they differed they discovered that their disputes had been settled as each had bowed to the Word of God. Oh that we might learn to settle our disagreements and divisions in a similar fashion!

But there is another aspect of this division. Division paralyses the fellowship of the church, to be sure, but more than that, *division publicises the membership of the church in its witness to the world.* 'For it hath been *declared* (an important word) unto me of you, my brethren, by them which are of the house of Chloe, that there are contentions among you.' Whether we like to admit it or not, there is no such thing as an isolated or insulated local church. Whatever happens inside becomes known outside. In terms of spreading the Gospel, this is one of the main functions of the local church; but, unfortunately, the same thing holds true when it comes to things we do not want to expose or disclose. So we find that division publicises the membership of the local church in a twofold manner.

Division adversely publicises *the name* of the church – 'For it hath been declared unto me of you, my brethren, by them which are of the house of Chloe.' Who Chloe was is not fully revealed to us, but with fair accuracy we can state that this wealthy lady, with her household, was known throughout the membership; and some of the servants of her household, travelling between Ephesus and Corinth, had brought the account of the divided state of the church to the attention of the apostle. So Paul takes pains to assert that what he had heard was not gossip or rumour. The Greek he employs signifies that his informant had made clear (or disclosed with accuracy) the sad situation. To confirm the report, Paul actually names Chloe and her household. If the apostle had learned of 'the contentions' in far off Ephesus, how about the rest of the church at Corinth; how about the believers in the environs, and how about the pagan world looking on?

Jesus taught His disciples that they were to be known by their love one towards another,[8] and it is on record that there were first-century Christians who loved one another in such a manner that the outside world stood back and said, 'See how these Christians love one another. Alas, alas, so many in the world stand back today, as they look at our local churches, and say, 'See how these Christians fight one another!' There can be no more adverse publicity to scandalise the membership of any church than news of division.

For many years it has been my privilege to conduct city-wide crusades throughout the British Isles, the United States of America and Canada, and I can testify without any fear of contradiction that when churches have united for Christian witness the spiritual impact has been tremendous: souls have been

[8] John 13:34-35

saved, saints have been edified, and 'times of refreshing' have been experienced from the presence of the Lord. On the other hand, when denominational differences or personal prejudices have characterised such efforts, the going has been hard, the results have been negligible, and the world has questioned the reality and relevance of the Christian message; and more likely than not, the press has carried adverse publicity.

But not only does division adversely publicise the name of the church, it also adversely publicises the *fame* of the church. I want to pick out a word in verse 11. Look at it carefully. 'For it hath been declared unto me ... that there are *contentions* among you.' The word 'contentions' is one which the apostle Paul uses in Galatians 5: 20 to condemn an ugly manifestation of the flesh. It denotes wrangling as opposed to orderly discussion, and leads to aroused feelings and shameful quarrels. Tragic as it is to state it, the Corinthian church was famous for this.

Without naming it, I know a church in the U.S.A. that was headlined in local and semi-national papers for 'splits' and 'schisms.' My heart just bled as I read the account, for I happen to know the history of that church – one that has dominated the entire state. Many missionaries have been sent out from that fellowship, but now it is divided down the middle, and the rival group has started another church while the rest of the members are floundering, trying to find themselves. The church has become famous, but *adversely* famous.

If Christians only knew it, this is exactly what

Satan is out to do in every local church. His mission is to disrupt, divide and destroy the Christian community. We join hands with the devil when we allow perverse activity to scandalise the membership. Whatever good a local church or congregation may do in the neighbourhood by way of witnessing for Christ, preaching the Gospel or visiting the homes, is eclipsed when there are quarrels, backbitings and contentions. If Christians would only recognise the irreparable damage done by division they would do everything in their power to maintain 'the unity of the Spirit in the bond of peace.'[9] Essentially we are one, because we are linked to the Father and the Son and the Holy Spirit, but it is our task to translate that unity into visibility by covering one another's failings with fervent love – so that the world never gets to know of our petty differences. [10]

Jonathan Goforth, in his book *By My Spirit*, writes of a revival in Korea in 1904 which literally swept thousands into the kingdom. It started, however, when he, as a senior missionary, was prepared to go to a fellow worker and apologise for harboured misunderstandings. As the two hearts were melted before God, the Holy Spirit was poured out as 'floods upon dry ground.'

But to proceed with our study, we must mark with soberness that division not only paralyses the fellowship and publicises the membership of the church, but also *polarises the leadership of the church in its witness to the world*. 'Now this I say, that every one of

[9] Ephesians 4:3
[10] 1 Peter 4:8

you saith, I am of Paul; and I of Apollos; and I of Cephas; and I of Christ.' There were some wonderful leaders associated with the church at Corinth, and their ministry had been unmistakably owned of God; but through dissension among the members the leadership was polarised in two ways.

First, there was devotion to men rather than the Master – 'Now this I say, that every one of you saith, I am of Paul; and I of Apollos; and I of Cephas; and I of Christ.' Division in the church is usually an evidence that eyes have been turned away from our blessed Lord Jesus Christ to men. So we find that four parties had emerged.

There were those who said they belonged to Paul and constituted the liberalistic party. You see, Paul had preached the Gospel of liberty. His message was: 'Stand fast therefore in the liberty wherewith Christ hath made us free, and be not entangled again with the yoke of bondage.'[11] It is most likely, therefore, that the members of this group were primarily Gentiles who had attempted to turn Christian liberty into carnal license. This was their excuse to do what they liked.

There were those who said they belonged to Apollos and constituted the philosophic party. Apollos was the product of the famous schools of Alexandria and, therefore, an essential philosopher at heart. He was master of the intellectual approach, the allegorical presentation and the rhetorical delivery. As a preacher, he was 'mighty in the scriptures'[12] and, consequently,

[11] Galatians 5:1
[12] Acts 18:24

made a strong appeal to the intellectuals of Corinth – with comparisons unfavourable to the apostle Paul.

There were those who said they belonged to Cephas and constituted the legalistic party. Cephas as you know, is the Jewish form of the name Peter. This group was made up of Hebrew Christians who maintained that a person must observe the Jewish law. These people regarded Peter as preeminent among the twelve disciples of the Lord Jesus Christ, and, therefore, supreme amongst the apostles. The fact that Paul had to withstand Peter at one point[13] was commonly known, and for this reason some were antagonistic to him.

Then there were those who claimed they belonged to Christ and constituted the separatistic party. This was a self-righteous sect who posed as if they were the only true Christians in Corinth. Their real fault was not in saying they belonged to Christ but in acting as if Christ belonged to them alone.

Now from a very careful study of this passage, it seems clear to me that while the parties may have had some theological differences, the main issue on which they were divided was not one of principle but one of personality. So unbalanced had they become in their devotion to certain leaders that they dared to assert that they belonged to them. In other words, they were guilty of the most damaging personality cult; and sad to say, this is one of the great problems in the Christian world today. Our churches are polarised by factions and followers that are associated with so-called 'big names.' Because one leader holds a certain

---

[13] Galatians 2:11

position while his opposite number takes a different stance, their respective 'disciples' invariably overreact and cause division. As believers, we seem to know so little of the inner strengthening of the Spirit to 'comprehend *with all saints* what is the breadth, and length, and depth, and height... (of) the love of Christ.'[14]

Therefore we find Paul in the following verses asking with evident indignation: 'Is Christ divided? was Paul crucified for you? or were ye baptised in the name of Paul?' The whole purpose of these penetrating questions was to show the utter absurdity, if not blasphemy, of lowering the Person of the Lord Jesus Christ to the level of human leadership. Paul was underscoring the fact that Christ is Head, not only of the total church, but also of the local church; and only as this is acknowledged can human leadership be authorised and recognised.

The passage goes on to say that the church was polarised, not only by devotion to men rather than the Master, but also by attention to messengers rather than the message. Paul says, 'I thank God that I baptised none of you, but Crispus and Gaius; lest any should say that I had baptised in mine own name. (I did baptise also the household of Stephanas. Beyond that, I do not know whether I baptised anyone else.) For Christ sent me not to baptise, but to preach the gospel.' In their carnality and divisiveness, these Corinthians had become so attracted to the messengers of the Gospel that they had forgotten the message of the Gospel. They were more impressed with the

[14] Ephesians 3:18–19

sacraments than they were with the Scriptures, more involved with the ordinances than with obedience. So Paul states with an obvious sense of relief, 'I thank God that I baptised none of you, but Crispus and Gaius.' In saying this, the apostle was not belittling baptism. In fact, the people Paul had baptised were very special converts – as a study of their names reveals; but so prone were these Corinthians to give personal allegiance to the one who baptised that they had overlooked the importance of the message that Paul had preached. I state again that in no sense was Paul seeking to minimise the sacred ordinances or the style of preaching; his burden was to turn the attention of the Corinthians away from the messengers to the message. The Christ into whom a person is baptised is more important than the ordinance; the message of the Gospel is more important than the method of delivery. As John Stott has written: 'All Christian work is fraught with great peril, and none more so than that of the Christian ministry. It is possible to engage in the ministry of the Word and sacraments, to preach and to baptise in such a way as to attach men and women to ourselves instead of to Christ ... The Word and sacraments bear witness to Christ. Preaching is the proclamation of Christ crucified. Baptism is baptism into the name of Christ crucified. We must exalt Christ in both, not men; the person who matters is not the one who preaches but the One who is preached; not the one who baptises but the Christ into whom we are baptised.'

So the ultimate remedy for a divided church is a return to the centrality of the Lord Jesus Christ. Paul emphasises this right throughout the opening paragraphs of this epistle. In fact, I invite you to take your pen or pencil and underscore the name of the Lord Jesus every time it is mentioned in the first seventeen verses. I think that you will find that in this short paragraph Christ is mentioned fourteen times! You see, the Corinthians had decentralised the Christ, and so had divided the church. Paul, therefore, brings them back to the Name of the Lord Jesus Christ, the One into whom they had believed, the One into whom they had been baptised. Thus for a fellowship that is paralysed, a membership that is publicised and a leadership that is polarised, the answer is ever and only Christ in all the glory of His Person and pre-eminence in the church. God had decreed that this is how it should be, if we are to know the fulness of heaven's benediction.[15]

Let us remember, however, that the local church is made up of individual Christians and that the issues that divide the membership are precisely the issues that divide my heart and yours. James, the apostle, convincingly argues this when he asks: 'From whence come wars and fightings among you? come they not hence, even of your lusts that war in your members?'[16] Where there is division in our hearts it is soon reflected in the fellowship, in the membership, and in the leadership. It follows, therefore, that before our witness can become effective to the world outside we have to become united inside, whether as a church or as individual Christians. This is what the Psalmist

[15] Colossians 1:18–19
[16] 4:1

means when he prays, 'Teach me thy way, O Lord; I will walk in thy truth: *unite my heart to fear thy name.*'[17] The united heart expresses itself in an unchallengeable life; and this is what the world is looking for today. This is why the Lord Jesus made such an impact upon His contemporaries. When people heard Him speak they were astonished at His authority. The secret was that His preaching and His practice were united. His character and His conduct were united. The unity of His heart was the essence of His authority. No one could question His devotion to God or His compassion towards men. There was no contradiction in His life or in His message.

As we conclude this study, I want to ask this very searching but simple question – are we religious contradictions or are we real Christians?

Seldom have I been so challenged as by a missionary couple who had just returned from the Democratic Republic of Somali. In her report, the young wife told of the severe restrictions on the proclamation of the Gospel and the distribution of Christian literature. She explained that even in conversation she was not allowed to discuss Christianity, unless directly asked for 'a reason of the hope that was in her.' Then she added quietly: 'In the Democratic Republic of Somali, my life must demand a supernatural explanation, or there is no chance to witness, no Christ to offer. In other words, my life is my message, and *what I am counts far more than what I say.*'

If you and I were placed in similar circumstances would our lives contradict the Gospel or would they

[17] 86:11

commend the Gospel? What contribution are you making? What contribution am I making to a world that is watching and waiting for a demonstration of unchallengeable Christianity? Can you and I say 'My life is my message'?

The Character of the Christian Message

I Corinthians 1:18-25

Contemporary Revolutions in our World
1. Revolution of a spiralling technology
2. Revolution of a rising expectation
3. Revolution of an emerging generation
4. Revolution of a changing culture
5. Revolution of a declining religion

1. THE CHRISTIAN MESSAGE IS GOD'S DISTINCTIVE REVELATION TO MAN (v. 18)
    1. The Wisdom of God with the Wisdom of man (v. 24)
        a. The Wisdom of God (v. 30)
            (i) The Revelation of Christ as our Righteousness (v. 30)
            (ii) The Revelation of Christ as our Sanctification (v. 30)
            (iii) The Revelation of Christ as our Redemption (v. 30)
        b. The Wisdom of Man (v. 21)
            (i) Human Wisdom is Earthly (v. 21)
            (ii) Human Wisdom is Sensual (v. 22)
            (iii) Human Wisdom is Devilish (vv. 19-20)

2. The Power of God with the Power of Man (v. 24)
   a. The Power of God (v. 18)
      (i) The Power by which Christ Came
      (ii) The Power by which Christ Lived
      (iii) The Power by which Christ Died
      (iv) The Power by which Christ Rose
      (v) The Power by which Christ Saves
   b. The Power of Man (v. 22)
      (i) The Scientific Approach to Things Spritual is Inadequate
      (ii) The Scientific Approach to Things Spiritual is Impertinent

II. THE CHRISTIAN MESSAGE IS GOD'S REDEMPTIVE INVITATION TO MAN (v. 24)
   1. God's Pleasure in the Invitation of the Gospel (v. 21)
   2. God's Purpose in the Invitation of the Gospel (v. 18)
   3. God's Process in the Invitation of the Gospel (vv. 21, 24)

2

THE CHARACTER OF THE CHRISTIAN MESSAGE

In our last study we were thinking about the Contradiction of the Christian Message, as reflected in a divided and, therefore, defeated church. By way of contrast, we now turn to a subject of infinite wealth and worth. In brief it is The Character of the Christian Message. Read with me I Corinthians, Chapter 1, verses 18–25.

> For the preaching of the cross is to them that perish, foolishness; but unto us which are saved, it is the power of God.
>
> For it is written, I will destroy the wisdom of the wise, and will bring to nothing the understanding of the prudent. Where is the wise? where is the scribe? where is the disputer of this world? hath not God made foolish the wisdom of this world? For after that in the wisdom of God the world by wisdom knew not God, it pleased God by the foolishness of preaching to save them that believe.
>
> For the Jews require a sign, and the Greeks seek after wisdom: But we preach Christ crucified, unto the Jews a stumblingblock, and unto

the Greeks foolishness; But unto them which are called, both Jews and Greeks, Christ the power of God, and the wisdom of God. Because the foolishness of God is wiser than men; and the weakness of God is stronger than men.

As we address ourselves to these verses it is my prayer that young and old alike will discover, with a new sense of wonder, the character of the Christian message. The times may change on earth, but the truth is forever settled in heaven. Speaking of 'the times,' we need to understand the days of revolution, or change, in which we live. This helps us to be intelligent and relevant in our presentation of the Gospel. So before we come to the exposition and application of this next section of the epistle, let us briefly survey the contemporary scene.

Some time ago, a penetrating writer made some observations in *Fortune* magazine which were rather striking and significant. He pointed out that we are living in the revolution of a spiralling technology. No thoughtful person can witness the advances that are being made in the field of technology today without feeling somewhat apprehensive. There are some very exciting things that are happening, but there are others that are disturbing. We know, for instance, that we have the potential to wipe out the human race. We are told, moreover, that within a matter of years it will be possible to determine breeding patterns and, therefore, to produce all types and complexes of people within our modern society. Quite naturally, we cannot reflect on data like this without becoming a little frightened.

THE CHARACTER OF THE CHRISTIAN MESSAGE

We are living in the revolution of a rising expectation. What is publicised on Madison Avenue today is what we expect to acquire at once. Failure to realise this has become one of the most frustrating problems of our day. Everything is instant: instant tea, instant coffee, instant postum, instant wealth, and so on, and people become very impatient when they do not get what is advertised. Moreover, what is true of the advertisements that we read in the newspapers, hear on the radio and see on television is equally true of the promises that are made by politicians, employers, teachers, and even parents. This is an age of expectation, and old and young have become intolerant when there is a delay in personal or practical fulfilment.

We are living in the revolution of an emerging generation. There is what has come to be called 'the generation gap,' and while I know that this is often overstated, I want to underscore something which is tremendously important in this regard. While there has been a generation gap in every century, there is something quite different about the present situation. Through mass communication and modern education, young people seem to have grown up overnight. Distinctives that existed before between parents and their children have now become issues to fight about. In this emerging generation there is no longer a threat to moral authority on the basis of revolutionism but rather on the ground of relativism. Today we are told that there are no absolutes; therefore, such terms as discipline, devotion and commitment are symbols of an establishment that must be overthrown.

We are living in the revolution of a changing culture. Culture is the public expression of national mentality and morality. To thoughtful people, it is quite obvious that our mentality is explosive and our morality is permissive. Our mentality is explosive because we are living in a day of interrogation and investigation. Children, young people, and adults are asking questions about everything. They want answers to such burning issues as racism, hunger, oppression, pollution, population explosion, and so on. We want answers, they say, don't talk to us in clichés; don't give us pious jargon; we want real answers. No longer can we silence the voices that protest and cry out against the injustices and indecisions of our time. But alongside of this is the morality which is permissive. Through the preaching of what Dietrich Bonhoeffer calls 'cheap grace' our liberal theologians have created a climate of antinomianism—not only within the church, but in society as a whole. 'Situation ethics' has become a way of life. The Ten Commandments, which were once an unalterable charter for personal and national behaviour are now relative, in terms of their application to modern life. We are told to regard the Ten Commandments as a rule of thumb for human convenience rather than divine insistence. We are informed that God's laws should be read as follows: 'Thou shalt not take the Name of the Lord thy God in vain *ordinarily*. Thou shalt not commit adultery *ordinarily*. Thou shalt not steal *ordinarily*. Thou shalt not bear false witness against thy neighbour *ordinarily*, and this, in turn, has led to unbelievable permissiveness in our society.

THE CHARACTER OF THE CHRISTIAN MESSAGE

Fornication, adultery, homosexuality, lesbianism, sodomy, pornography, nudity are all part of the changing culture, and we are expected to tolerate all this in the interests of so-called beauty and art forms for human appreciation.

But most serious of all is that we are living in the revolution of a declining religion. All societies throughout the ages have asked two basic questions. The first is 'Why?', the second question is 'Why not?' Up until now people have turned instinctively to religion for answers to these questions; but, alas, we live in an hour when instead of answering these questions the church herself is asking them! One cynical professor has remarked, 'What was once a question "Why?" has now become an answer "Why not?"' Dr James Packer has asserted that 'at no time, perhaps, since the Reformation have Protestant Christians as a body been so unsure, tentative and confused as to what they should believe and do.'[1]

It is in such a context and climate as this that we are privileged to present a Gospel which is both timely and, hallelujah, timeless! I cannot think of any passage in the New Testament which more clearly delineates what I call The Character of the Christian Message than the verses before us. So let us turn with confidence to the exposition of the paragraph that we have assigned to ourselves.

I have two main headings and here is the first one: *the Christian message is God's distinctive revelation to man.* 'For the preaching of the cross is to them that perish, foolishness; but unto us which are saved, it is

[1] *God Hath Spoken* (London: Hodder & Stoughton, 1965), p. 9.

the power of God.' Paul's emphasis here is not so much on the presentation of the Gospel; that will come later, but on the Logos, the word of the Gospel, in contradistinction to the 'wisdom of words' mentioned in verse 17. His supreme objective is to point out the uniqueness of the Gospel as a revelation of the *wisdom* and *power* of God. You see, these two words were highly significant in the generation in which Paul wrote. The Greeks were ever seeking after wisdom, while the Jews were obsessed with power. Thus Paul delineates the distinctive character of the Gospel by contrasting the wisdom of God with the wisdom of man and then the power of God with the power of man.

First of all, the wisdom of God with the wisdom of man – 'Christ ... the wisdom of God.' This mighty evangelist, this great preacher of the Gospel, leaves us in no doubt as to what he means by the wisdom of God. Verse 30 says: 'But ... in Christ Jesus ... God is made unto us wisdom, and righteousness, and sanctification, and redemption.' The American Revised Standard Version renders this as follows: 'Christ Jesus, who was made unto us wisdom from God, both righteousness and sanctification, and redemption.' In other words, the wisdom of God is revealed in righteousness, sanctification and redemption. And in this world of synthesis and syncretism, it is supremely important that we understand what God has to offer. We must realise afresh that religion (in the natural sense) is man's attempt to seek after God, whereas revelation (in the spiritual sense) is God's arrival to seek after man.

THE CHARACTER OF THE CHRISTIAN MESSAGE

In the wisdom of God we have, first of all, the revelation of Christ as our righteousness – 'But ... in Christ Jesus ... God is made unto us ... righteousness.' In and through the Lord Jesus Christ – if we have repented toward God and put our faith in Jesus as Saviour – we can be made just before a holy God. This aspect of the Gospel answers the ancient question, 'How can a man be justified with God?'[2] Because the Lord Jesus Christ died for our sins and rose again for our justification[3] we can know the righteousness of God imputed to us. The only message that can make a man right is the Gospel. God starts with the individual because, as Professor Samuel Zwemer says: 'The man who goes out to change society is an optimist, but the man who goes out to change society without changing the individual is a lunatic.' God starts at the centre and moves to the circumference. He makes a man right with his Creator and then with his neighbour.

Next, we have the revelation of Christ as our sanctification – 'But ... in Christ Jesus ... God is made unto us ... sanctification.' We could never attain holiness in our own strength, but through the Saviour's indwelling, sanctification is accomplished in us day by day. This continuous work of grace sets us apart for the purpose of God in terms of Christian belief and behaviour. It means living out experimentally what we are essentially in Christ. This is the heart of our message. Stated simply, it means that you and I cannot live the Christian life. Indeed, it is

[2] Job 25:4
[3] Romans 4:25

impossible to live the Christian life. Nobody has ever lived it save the Lord Jesus Christ. But when we come in utter bankruptcy and fling ourselves at the foot of the cross, saying, 'Nothing in my hand I bring, simply to Thy cross I cling,' the Lord Jesus not only cleanses us by His precious blood and reconciles us to His Father-God, but He communicates to us His resurrection life by the Holy Spirit. So a wonderful thing happens: we become new creatures: old things pass away; all things become new, and we are indwelt by the saving life of Christ. He looks through our eyes, speaks through our lips, works through our hands, walks through our feet, loves through our hearts, works out His purpose through our human personalities, and we discover that there is no demand made upon our lives which is not a demand upon His life in us. What a Gospel!

Then we have the revelation of Christ as our redemption – 'But ... in Christ Jesus ... God is made unto us ... redemption.' This word means 'release' or 'deliverance.' In this particular context it is not only redemption from the penalty and power of sin but from the very presence of sin. It is the final act of God by which we are made to conform to Christ in all the wonder of His likeness and glory. This final act could happen before the close of this day! I feel that we are on the verge of that great event. What a wonderful thought!

This, then, is the distinctive revelation of God to man, namely, Christ our righteousness, our sanctification, our redemption. But I want to add – and we shall be seeing this more clearly later on – that this revelation is wholly outside of man's capacity to conceive or perceive what God has prepared for them that love Him. Only the Holy Spirit can interpret to us the wonder of this Christian message in all its faithfulness and fulness.

Now Paul turns to the wisdom of man – 'For after that in the wisdom of God *the world by wisdom knew not God.*' This means that the world by philosophy cannot know God; the world by sophistry cannot know God. The apostle Paul absolutely agrees with the writer James when he tells us that man's wisdom is 'earthly, sensual, devilish.'[4] Let us pause to interpret this evaluation of human wisdom within our immediate context and see how Paul and James concur in this respect.

Human wisdom is earthly – 'For after that in the wisdom of God the world by wisdom knew not God.' Paul is telling us here that human wisdom is bound by limitation; it is earthly. Indeed, he states that God in His wisdom has decreed that the world by human wisdom cannot know God. How this forever annihilates the notion that man by his own reasoning or intellectual attainments can find God, leave alone *know* God! Human education at its highest and best is hardly adequate. No wonder the French scientist and religious philosopher, Blaise Pascal, once exclaimed, 'The supreme achievement of reason is to bring us to see that there is a limit to reason.'

Human wisdom is earthly, but it is also sensual. This is why Paul, with a touch of irony, says, 'The Greeks seek after wisdom.' William Barclay reminds

[4] 3:15

us that 'originally the Greek word "sophist" meant "a wise man" in the good sense; but later it came to signify a man with a clever mind and cunning tongue, a mental acrobat, a man who with glittering and persuasive rhetoric could make the worst appear the better reason... It meant a man who gloried in a nimble and a cunning brain and in a silver tongue and in an admiring audience.'[5]

What was true of Paul's day is still true today. There is nothing which appeals to the sensual and carnal person like the so-called intellectual speaker, the sophisticated preacher, or the silver-tongued orator, simply because such a communicator can pour out torrents of high-sounding words that mesmerise people by sheer rhetoric. Young people, particularly, run hither and thither after such men instead of sticking to the bread-and-butter issues of the Gospel of our Lord Jesus Christ.

Human wisdom is earthly, human wisdom is sensual, but even more importantly, human wisdom is devilish. So Paul quotes God as saying: 'I will destroy the wisdom of the wise, and will bring to nothing the understanding of the prudent. Where is the wise? where is the scribe? where is the disputer of this world? hath not God made foolish the wisdom of this world?' Human wisdom is described as devilish because it is associated with the devil who fell by pride. There is nothing more abhorrent to God than philosophical arrogance or intellectual snobbery. Every movement which has undermined the authority of the Scriptures – call it what you will:

[5] *The Letters to the Corinthians*, p. 21

modernism, liberalism, existentialism, or humanism – is all part of this philosophical approach; and because of human pride, men seek to be identified with the famous names of these schools of thought in order to secure a status symbol – but God calls it devilish.

Recently my heart was deeply stirred by the testimony of Mr A. Lindsay Glegg of London, England (now in his nineties). Standing before a breathless throng of young and old he told how, as a university student, he was carried away by the preaching and teaching of a man who had left the 'impregnable rock of Holy Scripture' for the sands of philosophical speculation, and how God, in love and mercy, drew him back to Himself, back to the Word, back to the church, and back to Christian service. I thought of young people across Britain, America, and the rest of the world as he concluded with these words: 'Keep to the Bible, keep at the foot of the cross, keep close to your Saviour. Make much of His virgin birth, His Deity, His sinless life, His atoning death, His indisputable resurrection, His High Priestly ministry, His certain return as Judge and Lord of all.' But somebody says, 'If you talk like that and believe like that are you not committing intellectual suicide?' The answer is no, for with Pascal we must remember that 'the supreme achievement of reason is to bring us to see that there is a limit to reason.' Once we arrive at this point and submit to divine revelation *we then begin to use our reasoning powers as never before*. Then and only then can our minds be stretched and strengthened by the Holy Spirit to understand things from God's point of view.

So we have seen what Paul means by God's distinctive revelation to men in terms of wisdom. Having compared the wisdom of God with the wisdom of man, Paul now proceeds to contrast the power of God with the power of man. Look at verse 24 – 'Christ the power of God.' To understand the distinct contrast between the power of God and the power of man it is necessary for us to examine carefully the meaning behind Paul's use of these phrases. Consider, first, the power of God – 'The preaching of the cross ... unto us which are saved ... is the power of God.' When God brought creation into being He only had to speak a word, but when God brought redemption to pass He had to send His only begotten Son. So the expression 'the power of God' comprehends the total act of God in Christ by which He made redemption possible for a world of ruined sinners.

Notice the power by which Christ came. The incarnation of our Lord Jesus Christ was a supernatural act of God. This is clear from the words of the angel to Mary: 'The Holy Ghost shall come upon thee, and the power of the Highest shall overshadow thee: therefore also that holy thing which shall be born of thee shall be called the Son of God.'[6] We observe, then, that it took nothing less than the exceeding might of divine power to effect this mystery of godliness. This is why I, Stephen Olford, believe in the virgin birth.

But with the power by which Christ came, think of

[6] Luke 1:35

the power by which Christ lived. The life of our Lord Jesus here upon earth was a supernatural act of God. Paul tells us that 'Jesus Christ our Lord ... was ... declared (or horizoned) to be the Son of God with power, according to the Spirit of holiness, by the resurrection from the dead.'[7] His sinless life is one of the greatest phenomena of the ages. I believe in His sinless life.

Then there is the power by which Christ died. The death of Christ was a supernatural act of God; for let us remember that when Jesus Christ hung upon the cross He was made sin for us in order that 'we might be made the righteousness of God in him.'[8] Then having completed His divine mission He voluntarily bowed His head and gave up the ghost. No one ever died like that. This is why Paul says, 'The (word) of the cross is ... the power of God.' I believe in His atoning death.

Next is the power by which Christ rose. The resurrection of the Saviour was a supernatural act of God. The apostle speaks of the 'exceeding greatness of (God's) power ... which he wrought in Christ, when he raised him from the dead.'[9] The resurrection of Christ is the foundation stone of Christian doctrine, it is the Gibraltar of Christian evidence, it is the Waterloo of infidelity and rationalism. If Christ did not rise from the dead our faith would be vain and we, of all men, would be most miserable. So I believe in the triumphant resurrection of Christ.

[7] Romans 1:3–4
[8] II Corinthians 5:21
[9] Ephesians 1:19, 20

Finally, there is the power by which Christ saves. The salvation of a sinner is a supernatural act of God. This is why Paul declares: 'I am not ashamed of the gospel of Christ: for it is the power of God unto salvation to every one that believeth; to the Jew first, and also to the Greek.'[10] At the very heart of the Gospel is the dynamic of God to save and to deliver. There is nothing else in all the universe which can transform human life like the Gospel of our Lord Jesus Christ.

I cannot read that verse without seeing a long-haired, moustached fellow, thirty years of age, David by name. He had been married twice, divorced twice. He had mainlined until his arms and legs were black and blue, but drugs had not satisfied him, and so he turned to alcohol until he became a complete outcast, even though the son of a Moody Bible Institute-trained father and mother. Having run away from home he headed for New York in search of new 'kicks.' One night he 'chanced' upon a TV programme when Arthur Blessitt was being interviewed along with some 'Jesus People.' He was so impressed with the joy and fervency of these recent converts to Christ that he longed to share their faith, so the following Sunday he turned on his TV, hoping to see something similar. Instead, however, he saw six lesbians and heard them tell of their sordid experiences. Even in his degraded state he could not take this, so he switched to another programme which, in God's providence, was our own Gospel presentation called ENCOUNTER. Through this

[10] Romans 1:16

means he was gloriously saved! Now he is in training for Christian service. Only the Gospel could do that!

If that is the power of God, let us take a moment on the power of man. 'The Jews,' says Paul, 'require a sign,' and, as Dr Leon Morris explains, this insistence on scientific proof has been characteristic of the Hebrew people throughout their history. They have shown little interest in speculative thought; their demand has been for evidence. They have thought of God as manifesting Himself in history through miracles and wonders. This is why the Jews were forever seeking signs from our Lord during His earthly ministry. They conceived of the Messiah as One who demonstrated His authority by manifestations of power and majesty. To them, a crucified Christ was a contradiction in terms.[11]

This, of course, illustrates perfectly the so-called scientific method which proceeds from observation through experimentation to demonstration. So men tell us that Christian supernaturalism must be rejected because it is inconsistent and incompatible with scientific knowledge. Suffice it to say, however, that such an outlook is both inadequate and impertinent. The scientific approach to things spiritual is inadequate. The apostle affirms this in a classic passage in Romans 10 when he says: 'The righteousness which is of faith speaketh on this wise, Say not in thine heart, Who shall ascend into heaven? (that is, to bring Christ down from above;) Or, Who shall descend into the deep? (that is, to bring up Christ again from the dead.) But what saith it? The word is

[11] *I Corinthians* (London: The Tyndale Press, 1958), p. 45.

nigh thee, even in thy mouth, and in thy heart: that is, the word of faith, which we preach; that if thou shalt confess with thy mouth the Lord Jesus, and shalt believe in thine heart that God hath raised him from the dead, thou shalt be saved.'[12] In other words, man cannot lift a little finger to bring Christ down from heaven, nor can he do any more to raise Christ from the grave. God has had to take the initiative at every stage of man's redemption. This is why the Gospel is so unique; and this is why the scientific approach to things spiritual is wholly inadequate.

But more than this, the scientific approach to things spiritual is truly impertinent. So the apostle asks the stinging question: 'For who hath known the mind of the Lord, that he may instruct him?'[13] And in another place the apostle exclaims: 'Who art thou that repliest against God? Shall the thing formed say to him that formed it, Why hast thou made me thus?'[14]

So we see that the revelation of the Gospel is not only beyond man's philosophical approach but also beyond man's scientific method. Once a seeking soul has reached this point he is ready for what is the second characteristic of the Gospel of our Lord Jesus Christ. My first point was that the Christian message is God's distinctive revelation to man; the second is that *the Christian message is God's redemptive invitation to man.* 'But unto them which are called, both Jews and Greeks, Christ the power of God, and the

[12] vv. 6–9
[13] I Corinthians 2:16
[14] Romans 9:20

wisdom of God.' Here we see presented the perfect balance of the Gospel. God not only gives us a revelation of Himself, He also gives an invitation to Himself. This is more than human wisdom; this is more than human power.

Consider, first, God's pleasure in the invitation of the Gospel – 'It pleased God by the foolishness of preaching to save them that believe.' Paul tells us here that the supreme pleasure of God, or more literally, God's good pleasure, is that men and women should be brought to a saving knowledge of Himself through preaching. Observe, carefully, that it is God who takes the initiative. The picture is not of man searching after God, but rather God seeking after man in all his lostness. Ever since Adam bowed to the voice of personified sin God, in grace, has been asking, 'Adam, where art thou?' 'Adam, where art thou?'

Furthermore, there is God's purpose in the invitation of the Gospel – 'For the preaching of the cross is to them that perish, foolishness; but unto us which are saved, it is the power of God.' Let us remember that every man out of Christ is lost. Indeed, the verb rendered 'perish,' in verse 18, denotes not extinction but ruin and loss of well-being. A person who is perishing fails to fulfil the purpose for which God created him; but this is where the Gospel of the Lord Jesus Christ meets him and saves him unto eternal life. The idea behind this word 'saved' is not only that of reclamation but also of transformation.

Then notice the process of God in the invitation of the Gospel. Not only His pleasure, not only His purpose, but the process of God in the invitation of the Gospel – 'It pleased God by the foolishness of preaching to save them that believe.... But unto them which are called ... Christ the power of God, and the wisdom of God.' There are two words that sum up the divine process in the invitation of the Gospel. The one is the word 'called,' and the other is the word 'believe.' The one describes the offer of God: He calls; it is His effectual call. The other denotes the response of man: he believes, he commits himself. Jesus is always calling men and women to Himself and, thank God, out of every tribe, tongue and nation men are responding. Wherever the Holy Spirit works and woos, men and women respond. That is the glorious process: God calls and man believes. I am glad that God called me to be an evangelist! There is nothing more thrilling in all the world than to issue the call of the Gospel and to see men and women believe. So we observe that this redemptive invitation of God demands a verdict. Man can never confront the Gospel of the Lord Jesus Christ and remain indifferent, apathetic or aloof. He has to decide. With the revelation and invitation of the Gospel man has to give an answer. If he believes he is saved; if he rejects he is lost.

The Corinthian believers were divided because they had false notions concerning this glorious message of the Gospel. This is why Paul takes pains in this first paragraph to set forth the character of the evangel; and having treated his subject thoroughly, he concludes with these words: 'The foolishness of God is wiser than men; and the weakness of God is stronger than men.' In effect, He says that the philosophies and power demonstrations of men may come and go, but the Gospel of Jesus Christ is unchanged and unchanging.

As I think of and thrill at the timelessness of our glorious message, I am reminded of the occasion when Carl Henry, then Editor-in-Chief of *Christianity Today*, attended a press conference called by Dr. Karl Barth. After some initial dialogue with other reporters, Dr. Henry took his turn and asked the famous theologian how he would have written up the event of the resurrection of Jesus Christ, had he been one of the early apostles. Stung by the question, Karl Barth played for time by snapping back with the demand, 'What religious journal do you represent?' The answer was swift and simple: '*Christianity Today*.' 'No,' retorted Barth, 'you mean "Christianity Yesterday."' Without hesitation, however, and with anointed insight, Henry countered with these choice words: 'You're wrong, Sir, it is rather "Christianity Yesterday, and Today, and Forever"!'

How wonderful to know that even though times may change truth is changeless and unchanging! Our Gospel is the same yesterday, today, and forever. Hallelujah!

The Community of the Christian Message

I Corinthians 1: 26–31

I. GOD SELECTS HIS COMMUNITY OF WITNESSING SAINTS THROUGH THE SIMPLICITY OF THE CHRISTIAN MESSAGE (v. 26)
   1. The Selective Simplicity of the Gospel does not appeal to many people of Intellectual Attainments (v. 26)
   2. The Selective Simplicity of the Gospel does not appeal to many people of Influential Achievements (v. 26)
   3. The Selective Simplicity of the Gospel does not appeal to many people of Inter-social Advancements (v. 26)

II. GOD ELECTS HIS COMMUNITY OF WITNESSING SAINTS THROUGH THE SUPREMACY OF THE CHRISTIAN MESSAGE (vv. 27–28)
   1. God Has Chosen to Save Foolish Humanity (v. 27)
   2. God Has Chosen to Save Feeble Humanity (v. 27)
   3. God Has Chosen to Save Fallen Humanity (v. 27)

III. GOD PROTECTS HIS COMMUNITY OF WITNESSING SAINTS THROUGH THE SUFFICIENCY OF THE CHRISTIAN MESSAGE (v. 30)
  1. Righteousness to Cover our Past (v. 30)
  2. Sanctification to Cope with our Present (v. 30)
  3. Redemption to Care for our Future (v. 30)

3

THE COMMUNITY
OF THE CHRISTIAN MESSAGE

We turn, next, to what I am calling The Community of the Christian Message. The Christian message is not an intangible ideology. The Christian message is essentially 'the Word of God incarnate.' The Apostle John makes this clear in that magnificent prologue to his Gospel. He says: 'In the beginning was the Word, and the Word was with God, and the Word was God.'[1] We would not know anything about God save for that Word. But for that Word to become humanly comprehensible it had to be 'fleshed out.' So we read: 'The Word (became) flesh, and dwelt (or tabernacled) among us, (and we beheld his glory, the glory as of the only begotten of the Father,) full of grace and truth.'[2] Mark carefully the clarity and symmetry of this interpersonal revelation. Grace reflects the curved lines of revelation while truth projects the straight lines. Here we see the glory of divine artistry. We need grace and truth to have the perfect balance, and in 'the only begotten of the Father' we have this

[1] John 1:1
[2] John 1:14

perfect balance of love and light. As one theologian has put it: 'Jesus Christ (became) God's conversation with men.' This was God's climactic invasion into community life upon earth. What happened vertically is now being worked out horizontally by God's Spirit through people like you and me. This is the community of the Christian message.

With that introduction let us read together I Corinthians 1: 26–31 and notice the imperative mood here; it is rather important:

See your calling, brethren, how that not many wise men after the flesh, not many mighty, not many noble, are called: But God hath chosen the foolish things of the world to confound the wise; and God hath chosen the weak things of the world to confound the things which are mighty; And base things of the world, and things which are despised, hath God chosen, yea, and things which are not, to bring to nought things that are: *That no flesh should glory in his presence.*

But of him are ye in Christ Jesus, who of God is made unto us wisdom, and righteousness, and sanctification, and redemption: That, according as it is written, He that glorieth, let him glory in the Lord.

The apostle is still dealing with the problem of division in the church. So he proceeds to show how strife and contention can result, not only from wrong notions concerning the character of the message of the Gospel, but also from wrong ideas concerning the community of the Christian message. In His divine sovereignty and inscrutable wisdom, God has so designed the appeal of the Gospel that men can merit absolutely nothing by responding to it. For this reason the community of the Christian message consists of a company of men and women who have learned that 'no flesh should glory in his presence.' No truly redeemed person can stand up and say, 'See who I am'; instead, he kneels to confess that 'Jesus Christ is Lord, to the glory of God the Father.'[3] God wants the world to see the glory of His Son through a community of saints in radiating beams of grace and truth.

It was because of the failure of the Corinthian Christians to see this that they were vying one against the other under the banners of their respective leaders. So Paul sets out to show that this problem can only be solved when people understand God's method of selecting, electing and protecting the community of believers in Jesus Christ.

Before we go any further, however, I think that it is important, especially for some of our younger friends, to recognise that the community of believers is, in fact, *the church*. We are living in an hour when people are saying that the greatest stumbling block to understanding the Christian message is the church! These people say 'we want Jesus, but we don't want the church.' You see how confused men and women have become! They see a dichotomy between Christ and the church, but there is no such dichotomy, for Christ is the Head of the church, and Christ calls the church His own Body. You will remember that when Saul of Tarsus persecuted the church of Jesus Christ

[3] Philippians 2:11

he was stricken down by a brilliant light, above the brightness of the meridian sun, and he heard a voice from heaven affirming, 'I am Jesus whom thou persecutest.' In other words, the Lord Jesus was saying, 'every Christian you are persecuting, every Christian you are hailing to prison, every Christian you are causing to blaspheme, is part of my Body, and *you are hurting Me*.'[4]

We need to be very careful, therefore, when we talk about the church, for while there are many things about the dead, cold, and irrelevant establishment which we must criticise and correct there is great caution required lest we actually insult or injure the very Body of Christ. If we are redeemed at all by the blood of Christ; if we are quickened at all by the Spirit of God; if we are taught at all by the Word of truth, then we are part of the church. Jesus said: 'I will build my church; and the gates of hell shall not prevail against it.'[5] There is a future for the church and, although her critics may come and go the church of Jesus Christ will endure forever.

With these thoughts in mind, let us return to the verses we read earlier and consider, in the first place, that *God selects His community of witnessing saints through the simplicity of the Christian message*. 'For ye see your calling, brethren, how that not many wise men after the flesh, not many mighty, not many noble, are called.' Later on in his second epistle, Paul expresses a fear 'lest by any means... the serpent... through his subtility ... should ... corrupt (the

[4] Acts 9, 22, 26
[5] Matthew 16:18

minds of the Corinthians) from the simplicity that is in Christ.'[6] The reason why people are being turned away from the church today is because so many Christians have ceased to be simple in their commitment to and contentment in Christ. This is why Paul invites us to survey the church and observe that those who constitute its membership are, for the most part, simple people.

The selective simplicity of the Gospel does not appeal to many people of intellectual attainments – 'Not many *wise* men after the flesh ... are called.' This is not because Christianity is anti-intellectual, as we shall see later, but because there is a natural tendency in the unregenerate person to *think* independently of God, as we observed so clearly in our last study. This is why the Lord Jesus declared: 'Except ye be converted, and become as little children, ye shall not enter into the kingdom of heaven.'[7] And on another occasion He looked up to heaven and said: 'I thank thee, O Father, Lord of heaven and earth, because thou hast hid these things from the wise (the philosophical) and prudent (the sophisticated), and hast revealed them unto babes. Even so, Father; for so it seemed good in thy sight.'[8] The fact of the matter is that Heaven has decreed that man, by his wisdom, his philosophy, and his knowledge, cannot know God. This unqualified repudiation of the philosophical approach to eternal things is in order 'that no flesh should glory in his presence.'

[6] II Corinthians 11:3
[7] Matthew 18:3
[8] Matthew 11:25–26

Nobody will ever be able to say, 'Thank God I am in Heaven because my brain has brought me here.' The selective simplicity of the Gospel does not appeal to many people of intellectual attainments. They have to repent; they have to change their thinking and submit to God's way of salvation.

It is also clear that the selective simplicity of the Gospel does not appeal to many people of influential achievements – 'Not many *mighty* ... are called.' There is a natural tendency in the unregenerate not only to think independently of God but to *work* independently of God. The word 'mighty' is a term used of people who have gained a place of influence through their own achievements. Now unless this pride of influence is 'crucified with Christ' there is always lurking trouble in the church. We are all familiar with a character in the church of Ephesus who caused unspeakable heartache. His name was Diotrephes, and his love of preeminence created nothing but strife and contention.[9] Indeed, because of his place of influence he had attacked the apostle John with 'malicious words.' In fact, there are scholars who tell us he had actually intercepted a letter to the Ephesian church. There is also a strong implication that he had tried to rival the authority of the aged and loved apostle. All this serves to illustrate the corrupting influence of uncrucified power, and for this very reason 'not many mighty are called.' God has willed it so in order 'that no flesh should glory in his presence.' Nobody can say when he gets to Heaven, 'I came here by means of my own works.'

[9] III John 9–11

The Bible says: 'Not by works of righteousness which we have done, but according to his mercy he saved us.'[10]

But once again, the selective simplicity of the Gospel does not appeal to many people of inter-social advancements - 'Not many *noble* are called.' There is a natural tendency in the unregenerate person to *live* independently of God. Most commentators are agreed that the word 'noble' applies to family connections and indicates those of high social standing. While there are outstanding exceptions, as we shall see in a moment, it is true to say that very few people of noble rank ever seem to be attracted by the Christian message.

In Paul's day, as in every age, there were the exceptions. There were such great personalities as Dionysius and Damaris of Athens,[11] Sergius Paulus, proconsul of Cyprus,[12] the noble ladies of Thessalonica, the noble ladies of Berea,[13] and not least, of course, the apostle himself, who were called into the fellowship of God's Son. Since then we could talk about a host of others - people like Count Zinzendorf and Madame Guyon - who came from nobility. Lady Huntington, an English woman of great distinction who was converted under the preaching of Rowland Hill, the evangelist, once remarked that she owed her salvation to the letter 'M.' By way of explanation she went on to add that if the text had

---

[10] Titus 3:5
[11] Acts 17:34
[12] Acts 13:7
[13] Acts 17:4, 12

read, 'Not *any* wise, not *any* mighty, and not *any* noble' she could never have been saved; but the text does not say 'any,' it reads 'not *many*'! There have been some noble people saved in the past, and there will be others in the future, until the church of Jesus Christ is complete; but notwithstanding this, the fact remains that by and large the simplicity of the Gospel does not appeal to those of inter-social advancements. Once again, God has willed it so in order 'that no flesh should glory in his presence.'

Anyone with a knowledge of the congregational life of a church will know that, very often, contention and division are caused through the desire and determination of some to have human recognition. It is only when we realise that we cannot think or work or live apart from God that true humility and consequent harmony come into the local fellowship. May the Spirit of God teach us to say and mean:

> Naught have I gotten but what I received;
> Grace hath bestowed it since I have believed.
> JAMES M. GRAY

This brings us to consider, in the second place, that *God elects His community of witnessing saints through the supremacy of the Christian message.* 'God hath chosen the foolish things of the world to confound the wise; and God hath chosen the weak things of the world to confound the things which are mighty; and base things of the world, and things which are despised, hath God chosen, yea, and things which are not, to bring to nought things that are.' To teach man forever that no flesh should glory in His presence, God has designed that His electing grace should demonstrate the utter supremacy of the Gospel. In other words, God has chosen to save foolish humanity – 'But God hath chosen the *foolish* things of the world to confound the wise.' The word Paul employs to describe humanity here is one from which we derive our term 'moron.' It is a word which means 'sluggish,' 'silly' or 'stupid.' But in His grace, God takes up material like this and transforms it by the redeeming work of Christ, so as to confound the wise of this world. Human philosophy can never explain the miracle of regeneration. The psychologist may attempt his analysis, the doctor his diagnosis, the scientist his experimentation, but ultimately all are confounded by the life-changing power of the Gospel.

Some years ago after our Sunday evening evangelistic service at Calvary Baptist Church, New York City, a very distinguished gentleman sought me out and asked if he could have a word with me. We sat down and he began: 'What you have had to say tonight has made sense. It is both reasonable and acceptable and I must act upon it. I want the Lord Jesus Christ to come into my life. I desperately need Him.' I did not even ask his name. I opened my Bible, expounded the way of salvation, and told him that the genius of the Christian message is that what we cannot do, in and of ourselves, God can do in us and through us. Christ died to make this possible, shed His blood to purge away our sins, rose again to impart His life, and stands waiting, though unseen to natural eyes, to enter our lives, and if only we invite Him in He always keeps His promise. 'Fair enough,' admitted my friend, 'I will ask Him in.' We bowed our heads together and he prayed a simple prayer, and in that moment Christ entered and possessed his personality.

With a smile on his face he extended his hand and was about to leave when I asked, 'Do you mind telling me who you are?' He replied, 'My name is Edgar Congdon, I am a doctor.' 'In what field?' I inquired. Graciously my friend explained, 'I started off in surgery, went into general medicine, and then I decided to become a psychiatrist.' I continued: 'As a psychiatrist, Dr Congdon, may I ask why you came here tonight?' His answer was both interesting and significant. Quietly he told me how he had always carried a chip on his shoulder. He looked down on Christians as morons and nitwits, and yet all the time he knew in his heart that he was 'the stupid idiot.' Although thoroughly qualified to analyse patients, prescribe medication, perform operations, give shock treatments, and so on, he had to confess that he had sent hundreds of patients away from his office without the real answer, because he did not have the answer himself. But then he added with a note of triumph in his voice, '*Now I have the answer!*' God has chosen to save foolish humanity, and we have to own our foolishness before we can know His salvation.

God has chosen to save feeble humanity – 'God hath chosen the *weak* things of the world to confound the things which are mighty.' Here is another characteristic of men and women who know nothing of the saving grace of God. Paul speaks of them as 'weak'

– a word which means 'strengthless' or 'impotent.' How wonderful to know, however, that 'when we were yet without strength, in due time Christ died for the ungodly'![14] And again: 'Not by works of righteousness which we have done, but according to his mercy he saved us, by the washing of regeneration, and renewing of the Holy Ghost.'[15] Man is powerless to work out his own salvation.

Never was this more evident than in our highly civilised age of technology. Philosophy has failed to answer the great questions concerning man's supernatural origin, his purpose on earth, his ultimate destiny. Likewise, the scientific method has proved to be totally inadequate to cope with man's basic problem of sin. With all the creations of his inventive mind, man has no computer and no machinery to change a man's character. If anything, he has produced more technological, psychological and theological problems than he has been able to solve. Once again, this is where the Gospel of our Lord Jesus Christ supremely triumphs by taking up the feeble and making them strong in the grace that God supplies through His eternal Son.

Then notice once again how God has chosen to save fallen humanity – 'And *base* things of the world, and things which are *despised*, hath God chosen, yea, and *things which are not*, to bring to nought things that are.' Here Paul introduces three expressions to describe the utter fallenness of man. 'Base things' conveys the thought of that which is low-born, and

[14] Romans 5:6
[15] Titus 3:5

therefore morally worthless; 'things which are despised' signifies that which is contemptible; 'things which are not' suggest the nonentities of this world. What a hopeless picture of fallen humanity! Yet the Lord Jesus by His saving cross receives and redeems such men and women and uses them to bring to nought things that are. Glory to God for such a Saviour!

So we see that the word of the Gospel has an instructive message for foolish humanity, a redemptive message for feeble humanity, and a creative message for fallen humanity; and out of all these three types of lost people God constitutes a community of saints and a community of witness.

Thus we see that there is no greater commendation for or demonstration of the Gospel than a person under the control of the saving life of Christ – like the old sailor who was so wonderfully converted and so visibly transformed that people kept on asking why his life-style was different. To answer this question he got his wife to knit him a sweater with the words 'Under New Management' in bold letters on the back and front! After that those three words became his 'text' for a five-minute sermon on the transforming power of the Gospel of Christ.

As we conclude this study, I must point out, how *God protects His community of witnessing saints through the sufficiency of the Christian message*. Paul says: 'But of him are ye in Christ Jesus, who of God is made unto us wisdom, and righteousness, and sanctification, and redemption.' For those who do respond to the selective and elective Gospel there is a protective sufficiency in the Gospel of Christ. The revelation of the wisdom of God, as seen in Jesus Christ, is made available to everyone of us, in terms of comprehensive significance.

There is righteousness to cover our past – 'Christ ... is made unto us ... righteousness.' This means justification in Christ. We attain a standing before God impossible otherwise or elsewhere. It is the assurance of pardon for sin and peace of heart. Isn't it wonderful to know that once the righteousness of God has been imputed to us we are before Him just as if we had never sinned? As justified persons, we are made to appear before God in a favourable light; and there is no angel in Heaven, there is no man on earth, and there is no devil in Hell who can challenge that! Here is our acceptance and assurance in Christ. So I ask you, have you been justified? Are you right with God?

Dr. Donald Barnhouse used to tell of a message he delivered in his church in Philadelphia on what God does with our sins. He pointed out that God has put our sins into the depths of the sea; He has put our sins as far as the east is from the west; He has put our sins behind His back, and so on and so on. At the end of the service, as he was shaking hands with members of his congregation, a little fellow with bright eyes, a sharp suit and an impressive bow tie, stood with consummate assurance before his pastor and exclaimed, 'Say, Doc', on the business of our sins, we are sitting pretty, aren't we?'

But with righteousness to cover our past, there is sanctification to cope with our present – 'Christ ...

is made unto us ... sanctification.' Dr. G. Campbell Morgan points out that sanctification is purification through separation.[16] It is both positional and practical. While it is true that 'by one offering (God) hath perfected for ever them that are sanctified,[17] it is equally true that we are to 'cleanse ourselves from all filthiness of the flesh and spirit, perfecting holiness (sanctification) in the fear of God.'[18] This progressive sanctification is the very life of Christ indwelling us moment by moment. And since all the fulness of the Godhead dwells bodily in our Lord Jesus Christ, there is no demand upon our lives which is not adequately met by the sufficiency which is in Him. It is our joy to rest in all that Christ not only has done for us, but also in all that He is in us. Evan Hopkins expresses this beautifully in those words we often sing:

> My Saviour, Thou hast offered rest:
> Oh, give it then to me;
> The rest of ceasing from myself,
> To find my all in Thee.

You show me a satisfied Christian; you show me a believer whose life is a sanctifying influence to the community around, and I will show you a person who has no problems in witnessing for Christ. The apostle Peter states the same principle when he says: 'Sanctify the Lord God in your hearts: and be ready always to give an answer to every man that asketh

---

[16] *The Corinthian Letters of Paul* (London: Charles Higham and Son, Ltd., 1947), p. 28.
[17] Hebrews 10:14
[18] II Corinthians 7:1

you a reason of the hope that is in you, with meekness and fear.'[19]

This sanctification is not only a personal power, it is a social power. As Christians, we are the salt of the earth; we are the light of the world.[20] So whether we are in business, in politics, in the home or in the church, we should be effecting a silent influence in society. We are the salt of the earth. But more than this, we should be effecting a vibrant radiance in society. We are the light of the world. Christians should be the strongest protesters against pornography, against nudity films, against the moral filth and political corruption of our day. As sanctified Christians, we should be speaking by life and by lip to the burning issues of our contemporary life. I am not contending for careless, tactless, or ruthless behaviour. I am not advocating unlawful assembly, or the violation of other civil regulations, for we, as Christians, are to submit to every ordinance of man for the Lord's sake,[21] but I am asserting that *our lives should be a challenge to everything that is wrong*.

There is, then, righteousness to cover our past, sanctification to cope with our present, and now redemption to care for our future – 'Christ ... is made unto us ... redemption.' As I mentioned in our previous study, redemption here means the final escape from all bondage. It is a word which occurs some ten times in the New Testament, and on every occasion it refers primarily to the future, rather than

[19] I Peter 3:15
[20] Matthew 5:13, 14
[21] I Peter 2:13

to the present or the past. Paul is speaking of the same things when he says, 'Now is our salvation nearer than when we believed.'[22] This is the sense in which Christ is made unto us redemption. This is the assurance of ultimate deliverance from sin, self and Satan. This is the day when He will fashion us into His own glorious likeness and loveliness. This is the sufficiency of the Christian message by which God protects the community of His witnessing saints.

Paul's purpose in presenting this truth was to remove forever from men's minds the thought of glorying in any other than God Himself – 'that, according as it is written, He that glorieth, let him glory in the Lord.' That which divides the church is the spirit that glories in human knowledge, glories in human influence, glories in human reputation. So the apostle has endeavoured to show that no one has anything to glory of, save in the Lord Jesus Christ. Man cannot think his way into salvation, he cannot work his way into salvation, he cannot live his way into salvation; he is cast on the mercy of God alone, and when he trusts in Jesus he simply becomes the vehicle through which the grace and truth of the Son of God shine forth in a blaze of beauty and glory. Then and only then is he a *message* to contemporary man.

John belonged to a club where language was coarse, standards were low, and tempers were short. One day he was invited by a young man with a radiant face to his local church, and then later to the Young People's Christian Fellowship. The welcome he received and the compassion he was shown deeply

[22] Romans 13:11

touched his heart. Then he heard the message of the Gospel, and by exercising repentance toward God and faith in the Lord Jesus Christ he was gloriously saved and miraculously transformed. As was to be expected, he left the club and began to attend the church, but it was not long before he was sought out by some of his old pals from the club who wanted to know why he had joined the church. John's answer was classic and conclusive. With a grin on his face and a nod towards the church, he said very simply: 'They loves a feller over there.' This is what Jesus meant when He said, 'By this shall all men know that ye are my disciples, if ye have love one to another.'[23]

The simplicity, the supremacy and the sufficiency of our message make this possible. This is the community of the Christian message. In our acts of worship and witness within our contemporary world we can either express this community of Christian living to the glory of God, or we can eclipse the outshining of Christ to our own confusion and condemnation. God give us the grace to 'walk worthy of the vocation wherewith (we) are called, With all lowliness and meekness, with longsuffering, forbearing one another in love; endeavouring to keep the unity of the Spirit in the bond of peace.'[24]

[23] John 13:35
[24] Ephesians 4:1–3

The Communication of the Christian Message

I Corinthians 2: 1–5

I. THE SUPREME PASSION OF A COMMUNICATOR (vv. 1–2)
    1. Dedication to the Master (v. 2)
    2. Concentration on the Message (v. 2)

II. THE SPIRITUAL POWER OF A COMMUNICATOR (vv. 3–4)
    1. The Power of Divine Revelation (vv. 3–4)
    2. The Power of Divine Application (vv. 3–4)

III. THE SINGLE PURPOSE OF A COMMUNICATOR (v. 5)
    1. A Sound Faith (v. 5)
    2. A Saving Faith (v. 5)
    3. A Steadfast Faith (v. 5)

4

THE COMMUNICATION OF THE CHRISTIAN MESSAGE

Now we come to The Communication of the Christian Message and for our text we look at I Corinthians, Chapter 2, verses 1–5:

> And I, brethren, when I came to you, came not with excellency of speech or of wisdom, declaring unto you the testimony of God.
>
> For I determined not to know any thing among you, save Jesus Christ and him crucified.
>
> And I was with you in weakness, and in fear, and in much trembling.
>
> And my speech and my preaching was not with enticing words of man's wisdom, but in demonstration of the Spirit and of power: That your faith should not stand in the wisdom of men, but in the power of God.

Having argued that the Christian message, while not commending itself to man's philosophical approach, is nevertheless the instrument of God's power and the complement of God's wisdom, Paul proceeds to discuss the communication of that message. There is nothing more important for businessmen and housewives, preachers and teachers, than this matter of communication. The priority programme of the church, until Jesus returns, is the communication of the Christian Gospel to every creature, in every country. The Master said: 'Go ye therefore and teach all nations, baptising them in the name of the Father, and of the Son, and of the Holy Ghost: teaching them to observe all things whatsoever I have commanded you: and, lo, I am with you always, even unto the end of the world.'[1] And again: 'Ye shall receive power, after that the Holy Ghost is come upon you: and ye shall be witnesses unto me both in Jerusalem, and in all Judea, and in Samaria, and unto the uttermost part of the earth.'[2]

As a communicator himself, Paul knew something of the inherent dangers in the methods and motives of public preaching. Indeed, the church at Corinth was divided on this very issue. Some said they preferred Paul, others said they preferred Apollos, still others said they preferred Cephas, and so on. There was division because of the differences and preferences relating to the personalities and presentations of these preachers. So Paul tackles this problem by saying, in effect, that temperament, background and training are not what matters; the anointing of the Holy Spirit is needed to be a communicator for Christ. This anointing of the Spirit concerns three aspects of the task as a communicator.

First of all, there is *the supreme passion of a communicator*. 'And I, brethren, when I came to you,

[1] Matthew 28:19–20
[2] Acts 1:8

came not with excellency of speech or of wisdom, declaring unto you the testimony of God. For I determined not to know any thing among you, save Jesus Christ, and him crucified.' Drawing heavily upon his own experience, Paul shares with us the twofold secret of the consuming passion of a Gospel communicator.

There is, to start with, dedication to the Master. Paul uses a special word here to describe his dedicated resolve. He says, 'I *determined* not to know any thing among you, save Jesus Christ.' This is the secret of a true passion for preaching and communicating. This man was so Christ-centred and Christ-controlled that nothing else mattered, save Jesus Christ. He could say, 'For me (living) is Christ';[3] and again:' I count all things but loss for the excellency of the knowledge of Christ Jesus my Lord... that I may know him, and the power of his resurrection, and the fellowship of his sufferings, being made conformable unto his death';[4] and yet again: 'This one thing I do, forgetting those things which are behind, and reaching forth unto those things which are before, I press (or I pursue; same word which he used for the persecution of the church) toward the mark for the prize of the high calling of God in Christ Jesus.'[5]

How true it is that 'out of the abundance of the heart the mouth speaketh'![6] Some of us remember the crusade that Dr Billy Graham had at Harringay in the city of London. I was then pastor of the Duke

[3] Philippians 1:21
[4] Philippians 3:8, 10
[5] Philippians 3:13–14
[6] Matthew 12:34

Street Baptist Church in Richmond, Surrey, and we took scores of people every night to the meetings. Riding home on one or two occasions by way of the Underground, I made it my business to go from car to car and meet people who had just trusted Christ. It was absolutely thrilling! These folk were so full of their newfound joy that they were singing and talking about Jesus in every compartment of the train. And it did not matter how much the conservative Britisher tried to hide his face in *The Times* or the *Telegraph*, he still had to hear. 'Out of the abundance of the heart the mouth speaketh.'

Many years ago I was preaching in the city of Birmingham, England, and while there stayed in the home of a lovely couple. Just before my arrival their daughter had become engaged, so almost the first word of greeting was, 'You know, Dorothy has become engaged!' I therefore turned to Dorothy and said, 'Tell me, who is he?' and she, with radiant face, replied, 'Oh, his name is George.' Well, you know, I thought that was the end of it. But believe me when I tell you that we had George for breakfast, George for lunch, and George for supper! At the table when Dorothy passed the sugar it was with the left hand, so that everyone could see those flashing facets of the engagement ring! You see, 'out of the abundance of the heart (and life) the mouth speaketh.'

A little later, in that same city, I was speaking at a rally on the theme of witnessing, and at the close of the meeting a young fellow came to me and said, 'You know, I find it difficult to speak about the Lord Jesus. I can talk about other things, but when it comes to witnessing for Christ I just seem to be tongue-tied.' I paused a moment and then put this question to him. 'Tell me,' I asked, 'have you a hobby?' 'Oh, yes!' he exclaimed, 'My hobby is motorcycling.' 'That is very interesting,' I observed, 'because I used to own a motorbike.' His eyes opened like saucers, and in a moment he had launched into a most detailed description of motorcycles in general, and his machine in particular. In fact, for twenty minutes I couldn't get a word in edgewise! Finally I stopped him and gave him this parting word: 'Son, when you spend as much time with Jesus as you do with your favourite hobby, you will have a polished twenty-minute sermon every time you speak!'

Dedication to the Master; this was Paul's passion. For him living was Christ. As the pages of the Old Testament Scriptures opened to him it was Jesus he saw. As he prayed it was Jesus he felt. As he witnessed to others it was Jesus he shared. So it should be with us. Our holiness, our power, our victory, our blessing, are all wrapped up in Christ, and if the Lord Jesus means everything to us, we cannot but talk about Him. Thus Paul could say, 'I determined not to know any thing among you, save Jesus Christ.'

But alongside of dedication to the Master there was concentration on the message – 'For I determined not to know any thing among you, save Jesus Christ, *and him crucified.*' Paul determined to present Christ in all the simplicity of the essential facts of His death and resurrection. His supreme passion was Christ and Him crucified. And knowing what the philosophers of Corinth stood for, he saw to it that his message was Christ and Him crucified – 'not in His glory but in His humiliation, that the foolishness of the preaching might be doubly foolish, and the weakness doubly weak. The incarnation was in itself a stumbling block; the crucifixion was much more than this.'[7]

Now some students of the Bible maintain that Paul's emphasis on the cross in the city of Corinth was because of his sense of failure in the alleged philosophical approach he adopted at Athens. But a study of Acts 17 makes it evident that the apostle's preaching there was not basically philosophical, even though he did quote from the philosophers of his day. His sermon began with a biblical presentation of creation and ended on the note of the resurrection. Why would he speak of the resurrection if there were no crucifixion? Whether in Athens or Corinth, Paul could affirm, 'I determined not to know any thing among you, save Jesus Christ, and him crucified.' The Gospel, according to Paul, was that 'Christ died for our sins according to the Scriptures ... he was buried, and ... he rose again the third day according to the Scriptures.'[8]

A young preacher in a college town was embarrassed by the thought of criticism that he was likely to receive from his cultured congregation. He sought out his father, an old and wise minister of the Gospel, and said, 'Father, I find it hard to outline a sermon that I can preach to these people. If I cite anything from geology, there is Doctor A – the geology pro-

---

[7] Bishop Lightfoot
[8] I Corinthians 15:3, 4

fessor before me. If I use an illustration from history, there is Doctor B – ready to trip me up. If I choose English literature for some allusion, I am afraid the whole English department will challenge me. What shall I do?' The sagacious and godly old man replied, 'Preach the Gospel, my son, they probably know very little about that!'

Tholuck adopted the motto of Count Zinzendorf – 'I have only one passion, and it is He, only He.' Martin Luther's preaching aroused the church from a thousand years of slumber, known by the historians as the devil's millenium. It is easy to understand why, when we discover how he preached. Luther said, 'I preach as though Christ was crucified yesterday, rose again from the dead today, and is coming back to earth tomorrow.' This is the supreme passion of the communicator – dedication to the Master and concentration on the message.

This brings us to our second point, which is *the spiritual power of a communicator*. 'And I was with you in weakness, and in fear, and in much trembling. And my speech and my preaching was not with enticing words of man's wisdom, but in demonstration of the Spirit and of power.' The apostle knew that the content of his message was so unacceptable to the carnal mind that he had no confidence in his ability to communicate it. In fact, he admits that he came to Corinth 'in weakness, and in fear, and in much trembling.' J. B. Phillips puts it even more dramatically when he renders Paul as saying, ' "I was feeling far from strong, I was nervous and rather shaky." '

Housewife, have you ever felt like that as you waited to purchase your 'weekend roast,' and the lady in front of you made a remark that gave you a wide open door to witness for Christ? Preacher, have you ever felt like that when you came on to the platform to deliver your sermon? I am encouraged by the words of Dr. G. Campbell Morgan when he confesses, in one of his writings, that every Sunday, as he made his way to the pulpit, he was invariably reminded of that Scripture, 'He (was) brought as a lamb to the slaughter.' I can honestly say that I have never preached in my life without experiencing 'butterflies' inside. Time and again, I have prayed, 'Lord, how am I ever going to get through this message?' And instead of less fear I was given more fear. Why? Surely it was God teaching me that it was not human oratory or human argument that was going to get the message across of a crucified and risen Saviour, but rather the Holy Spirit with quiet demonstration and power. So Paul says, 'I was feeling far from strong, I was nervous and rather shaky.' His fear, of course, was more of God than of man. It was a fear of the task committed to him, or what Kay calls 'anxious desire to fulfil his duty'; thus he writes: 'My speech and my preaching was not with enticing words of man's wisdom, but in demonstration of the Spirit and of power.' This means that Paul did not depend on what was known as 'the Corinthian words' of excellent speech and poetic persuasion; his confidence, rather, was in the power of divine revelation – 'I was with you in ... demonstration of the Spirit.' The word translated 'demonstration' signifies 'the most rigorous proof.' As Dr. Leon Morris puts it: 'It is possible for arguments to be logically irrefutable, yet totally unconvincing.'[9]

What, then, is the secret of preaching or communicating Christ? Paul tells us that it is the demonstration *of the Spirit*. When the Holy Spirit takes over the argumentation in the simple language of a housewife, a businessman, a schoolgirl, or a schoolboy, something miraculous happens. This is the essential difference between human reasoning and divine revelation. When communicators of the Christian message trust in their own powers to convince men and women 'of sin, and of righteousness, and of judgement' they miserably fail, but when they trust in the Holy Spirit there is always 'old-time conviction.' This is why Jesus said before He left for Heaven, 'When he (the Holy Spirit) is come, he will reprove (convince) the world of sin, and of righteousness, and of judgement: of sin, because they believe not on me; of righteousness, because I go to my Father ... of judgement, because the prince of this world is judged.'[10]

So we can be communicators of this glorious message of Christ and Him crucified because we have received the Spirit of revelation. Our bodies are the temples of the Holy Spirit.[11] The temple was the place of revelation, where God's word and will were made known. How wonderful to know, then, that you and I can be temples of revelation!

[9] *I Corinthians*, p. 52
[10] John 16:8–11
[11] I Corinthians 6:19

But there is not only the power of divine revelation, there is also the power of divine application – 'I was with you . . . in demonstration (this is the revelation) of the Spirit and of power.' The phrase 'of power' carries us back to the 'dynamic of God' in the words of the cross.[12] There is something inherent in the Gospel of our Lord Jesus Christ which has a dynamic relevance, and therefore an application to everyday living. Preach the Gospel to any creature, in any country, in any age, and you will find it just as authoritative and applicable as it was in the days of the apostle Paul. I have actually spoken by interpretation, when communication involved four or five languages, and people have been converted! This is the miracle of divine application. This is why Paul exclaims, 'I am not ashamed of the gospel of Christ: for it is the power of God unto salvation to every one that believeth; to the Jew first, and also to the Greek.'[13]

I suppose the most dramatic illustration of this is the young fellow I interviewed on our television programme. His name is Rick Carreno, formerly one of Hell's Angels – a club of motorcycle riders. He hesitates to speak about his past life, but suffice it to say that he was guilty of the most dreadful deeds of obscenity and cruelty that anyone could ever talk about. Eventually, however, he came to an end of himself. He tells how on a drug trip he climbed into a metal trash can, pulled the cover down, and determined to die. For four days he stayed in that self-imposed prison without light, food or hope. Then

---

[12] I Corinthians 1:18
[13] Romans 1:16

at the urging of his mother he attended a Billy Graham Crusade meeting. As he lay on the grassy infield, listening to the evangelist, the withdrawal pains got worse and he began to cry; he realised he was breaking down. The Spirit of God, through revelation and application, began to communicate the message to his heart, and Rick decided to give his life to something greater – Someone who could do the job he had failed to do. Very simply, he prayed and invited Christ to take control of his life, and instantly he was delivered from the desire for and power of drugs. Since then he has spent a year at Bible School and is now in evangelistic work. Such is the power of the Holy Spirit in the revelation and application of saving truth.

My last point is *the single purpose of a communicator*. 'That your faith should not stand in the wisdom of men, but in the power of God.' No communicator fulfils his mission until he brings boys and girls, men and women, to rest their faith in the power of God; and as we have observed already, the power of God is nothing less than the word of the Gospel, even our Lord Jesus Christ crucified and risen. The problem in Corinth was that the members of the church were seeking to pin their faith on Paul, or on Apollos, or on Cephas. So Paul takes pains to correct this divisive misplacement of confidence. To achieve this end, he realised that men and women had to exercise faith; and for faith to be sound the apostle knew that it had to be reposed in the Saviour Himself without dependence on human wisdom or power. Paul amplifies this point when he writes later concerning the death and resurrection of the Lord Jesus Christ in Chapter 15 of this same epistle. There he declares: 'If Christ be not raised, your faith is vain; ye are yet in your sins.'[14] If Christ were not alive from the dead then sin was not put away, the Gospel was not true, the Corinthians had believed a lie, the apostles were false witnesses, and the loved ones who had fallen asleep had gone forever. So to be sound in the faith a person must believe in the Son of God who literally and physically rose from the dead. All other tenets of evangelical faith are both included and implied in this one central and focal fact of the resurrection of Christ.

Let me pause here to ask some personal questions. Is your faith sound? Do you believe that Jesus Christ died and rose again for your justification? Have you a sound faith?

More than this, have you a saving faith? Does it stand in the power of God? Paul has explained the meaning of 'the power of God' in a previous verse. You will remember that he has asserted that 'the preaching of the cross is to them that perish, foolishness; but unto us which are saved, it is the power of God.' A saving faith is one which effects a mighty transformation in the believing soul. It is a faith which owns the Lord Jesus as Saviour in the deepest sense of that word. So I ask: can you sing –

He lives, He lives, Christ Jesus lives today!

He walks with me and talks with me along life's narrow way.

He lives, He lives, salvation to impart!

[14] I Corinthians 15:17

THE COMMUNICATION OF THE CHRISTIAN MESSAGE

You ask me how I know He lives?
He lives within my heart.

Alfred A. Ackley

Yes, you must have a sound faith, a saving faith, and also a steadfast faith – 'That your faith should not stand in the wisdom of men, but in the power of God.' It has been well said that what depends upon a clever argument is at the mercy of a more clever argument. But this is not so when faith is reposed in the unchanging Son of God. This is why Paul employs the term 'stand' which conveys the idea of steadfastness. Twice over in this epistle he exhorts the believer to be steadfast in the faith. The first mention follows the glorious treatment of the unalterable facts of the death and resurrection of our Lord Jesus Christ in Chapter 15. Having declared the triumph of the Saviour over sin and death and Hell, Paul says: 'Be ye steadfast, unmovable, always abounding in the work of the Lord, forasmuch as ye know that your labour is not in vain in the Lord.'[15] The second reference coincides with the conclusion of the epistle where the apostle exhorts: 'Watch ye, stand fast in the faith, quit you like men, be strong.'[16]

So we have examined what Paul means by The Communication of the Christian Message. He has made it abundantly plain that the Gospel of God cannot be communicated or understood apart from a God-given passion, a God-given power, and a God-

[15] I Corinthians 15:58
[16] I Corinthians 16:13

given purpose. Thus whoever claims to be a communicator must possess these qualifications through the sovereign grace of the Holy Spirit.

The famous British preacher, Rowland Hill, knew something of this. Addressing the people of Wootton during one of his pastorates he declared: 'Because I am earnest in my preaching men call me an enthusiast, a fanatic. When I first came to this part of the country I was walking on yonder hill and saw a gravel pit fall in and bury three human beings alive. I lifted up my voice for help so loudly that I was heard in the town below at a distance of nearly a mile. Help came and two of the sufferers were rescued. No one called me an enthusiast or a fanatic that day; yet when I see eternal destruction ready to fall upon poor sinners, and I call upon them to escape, men dare to call me an enthusiast and a fanatic. How little they know of my accountability to God and my responsibility to men!'

Never in human history have means of communication become more accessible and adaptable to the preacher of the Christian message. Today we have the printing machine, the pocket receiver, the television screen and transmission by satellite. In fact, we are told that the time will soon come when people will be able to view a television programme in any part of the world by means of a device as small as a wristwatch. Such facts as these should stir our hearts and strengthen our hands as we seek to preach the Christian message to every creature. Let us remember, however, that whatever means we may employ in this technological age, nothing can ever take the place of the personal witness of life and lip. Our daily prayer should be:

> Mine are the hands to do the work;
> My feet shall run for Thee;
> My lips shall sound the glorious news:
> Lord, here am I; send me.
>
> *Howard W. Guinness*

The Comprehension of the Christian Message

I Corinthians 2: 6–16

I. SPIRITUAL INITIATION (vv. 6–7)
   1. Spiritual Birth (v. 6)
   2. Spiritual Growth (v. 6)

II. SPIRITUAL ILLUMINATION (vv. 9–10)
   1. The Revelation of the Spirit (v. 10)
   2. The Exploration of the Spirit (v. 10)

III. SPIRITUAL INTERPRETATION (v. 13)
   1. The Spirit's Use of Language (v. 13)
   2. The Spirit's Terms of Reference (v. 13)
       The Law of Righteousness (Matthew 3:15)
       The Law of Yieldedness (Matthew 3:16)
       The Law of Prayerfulness (Luke 3: 21, 22)

5

THE COMPREHENSION OF THE CHRISTIAN MESSAGE

Our final message in this series of studies on The Christian Message for Contemporary Man is based upon I Corinthians 2: 6–16.

Howbeit we speak wisdom among them that are perfect: yet not the wisdom of this world, nor of the princes of this world, that come to nought: But we speak the wisdom of God in a mystery, even the hidden wisdom, which God ordained before the world unto our glory; Which none of the princes of this world knew: for had they known it, they would not have crucified the Lord of glory.

But as it is written, Eye hath not seen, nor ear heard, neither have entered into the heart of man, the things which God hath prepared for them that love him. But God hath revealed them unto us by his Spirit: for the Spirit searcheth all things, yea, the deep things of God.

For what man knoweth the things of a man, save the spirit of man which is in him? even so the things of God knoweth no man, but the

Spirit of God. Now we have received, not the spirit of the world, but the Spirit which is of God; that we might know the things that are freely given to us of God. Which things also we speak, not in the words which man's wisdom teacheth, but which the Holy Ghost teacheth; comparing spiritual things with spiritual.

But the natural man receiveth not the things of the Spirit of God: for they are foolishness unto him: neither can he know them, because they are spiritually discerned. But he that is spiritual judgeth all things, yet he himself is judged of no man.

For who hath known the mind of the Lord, that he may instruct him? But we have the mind of Christ.

Having dealt with the content and communication of the Gospel, the apostle now concludes with his paragraph on The Comprehension of the Christian Message. He anticipates those who might have inferred from his argument thus far that the use of the intellect is not in God's economy, which is, of course, far from the truth. For anyone in our day similarly misled I warmly commend John Stott's booklet, *The Mind Matters*, (published by I.V.F.). Paul deals with this issue by pointing out that the Christian message does contain philosophy, but that this system of thought is spiritual and therefore can only be comprehended by spiritual means.

There are three aspects of the Holy Spirit's ministry which enable us to comprehend the Christian message. The first is that of *spiritual initiation*. 'Howbeit we speak wisdom among them that are perfect: yet not the wisdom of this world, nor of the princes of this world, that come to nought: but we speak the wisdom of God in a mystery, even the hidden wisdom, which God ordained before the world unto our glory.' In effect, Paul is saying, 'Do not imagine that Christianity is devoid of philosophy, of wisdom, that it is something outside the realm of the (renewed) intellect. It is not. It has its own wisdom, its own philosophy, Indeed, what the apostle is showing here is that the Christian philosophy is the ultimate philosophy. It is *not* to be tested by other philosophies. They are to be tried by it. "We speak wisdom," he states...with (absolute) finality.'[1] And the wonderful thing about it is that this ultimate wisdom of God, as revealed in the Lord Jesus Christ, is for you and me by means of divine initiation.

Paul describes this wisdom as 'a mystery, even the hidden wisdom, which God ordained before the world unto our glory.' It is a wisdom which comes out of eternity, invades time, and lives on throughout the ages. This is why it is called 'a mystery,' and therefore only comprehensible to those who are spiritually initiated. The word 'mystery' signifies 'something whose meaning is hidden from those who have not been initiated, but which is crystal clear to those who have.'[2]

Now, of course, the question arises as to how you and I can be initiated, how we can be brought into this 'secret of God.' The answer is implicit in that

[1] Morgan, p. 33
[2] Barclay, p. 29

little word 'perfect.' Paul states: 'We speak wisdom among them that are *perfect*.' A careful examination of this passage makes plain that Paul equates those that are perfect with those that are spiritual; in other words, those who have the Holy Spirit dwelling in them and revealing to them the deep things of God. This means, then, that spiritual initiation involves a spiritual birth followed by a spiritual growth.

To start with, there must be spiritual birth – 'Howbeit we speak wisdom among them that are perfect.' The term 'perfect' denotes 'the full grown' or 'mature,' in contrast to the babe. Now before there can be development and maturity there must be spiritual birth. This was an essential element in our Saviour's ministry, especially when He confronted one of the most intellectual men of His day. Archaeologists inform us that this man, whose name was Nicodemus, was not only a theologian and a philosopher, he was also a *scientist*, for he engineered the waterworks in the city of Jerusalem! And it was to this man that the Lord Jesus said, 'Verily, verily, I say unto thee, Except a man be born again, he cannot see the kingdom of God.'[3]

There are people who say to me, 'We can't understand the Bible,' and invariably my answer is, 'You must be born again!' If Jesus had to say to this philosopher, this theologian, this scientist 'You must be born again before you can see the kingdom of God' what about you, my friend? Thank God, this miracle can happen in your life, if only you will receive the Lord Jesus. The Bible assures us that 'as many as

[3] John 3:3

received him (the Lord Jesus), to them gave he power to become the sons of God, even to them that believe on his name: Which were born, not of blood, nor of the will of the flesh, nor of the will of man, but of God.'[4] You see, you do not enter the kingdom of God by human descent; it is 'not of blood.' You do not enter the kingdom of God by human desire; it is not of 'the will of the flesh.' You do not enter the kingdom of God by human design; it is not of 'the will of man.' It is rather by an act of God in response to believing faith and receiving faith. So many people believe but do not *receive*. They have been brought up in religious circles all their lives – Presbyterian churches, Methodist churches, Baptist churches, Pentecostal churches, and so on – and they have believed, but they have never received the Lord Jesus Christ. Have you received Him? Have you been born again? Only by this spiritual birth can you be initiated into the mystery of the Gospel.

Spiritual birth leads to spiritual growth – 'Howbeit we speak wisdom among them that are *perfect*.' I have pointed out already that the word 'perfect' describes a person who has developed physically, mentally or spiritually. In this context Paul has in mind the idea of spiritual growth. Pythagoras divided his disciples into those who were babes and those who were perfect. In other words, he made a distinction between people who had gotten beyond the rudimentary instructions in the elements of any subject and those who were still beginners. Paul makes the same distinction when he addresses the spiritual and

[4] John 1:12–13

the carnal in the third chapter, verses 1–3.

One of the heartaches in church life today is that we have so many crying, bottle-sucking babies! It is about time Christians grew up. It is about time they changed their diet from milk to meat, for 'meat belongeth to them that are of full age.'[5] At this point it is appropriate to ask whether you have experienced this initiation of the Holy Spirit. Have you been born again, and are you growing?

But let us hurry on and observe that the comprehension of the Christian message involves not only spiritual initiation, but also *spiritual illumination*. 'But as it is written, Eye hath not seen, nor ear heard, neither have entered into the heart of man, the things which God hath prepared for them that love him. But God hath revealed them unto us by his Spirit: for the Spirit searcheth all things, yea, the deep things of God.' Following spiritual initiation there must be illumination, and the reason for this is that human contemplation and observation can never penetrate the deep things of God. In other words, the philosophical approach and the scientific method are limited by time and sense, and can only bring us to the end of human reasoning. But where human investigation fails, spiritual illumination prevails.

Thus Paul proceeds to show that if a person has qualified by spiritual birth and growth he can know the revelation of the Spirit – 'But God hath revealed (spiritual things) unto us by his Spirit.' To illustrate his point the apostle adds: 'For what man knoweth the things of a man, save the spirit of man which is in

[5] Hebrews 5:14

him? even so the things of God knoweth no man, but the Spirit of God.' What he is asserting is that there are certain things which only a man's spirit can know. Everyone of us is aware of this. No one can really see inside our hearts and know what is there except our own spirits.

From this premise Paul goes on to argue that the same is true of God. There are deep and intimate things about God which only His Spirit can reveal to us. Or to put it in another form: there are areas of truth that the unaided human mind can never find out, save through the illumination of the Holy Spirit. This is why the Lord Jesus, when leaving His disciples, promised them the Holy Spirit Who would teach them all things, and bring all things to their remembrance.[6]

But with the revelation of the Spirit there is also the exploration of the Spirit – 'For the Spirit searcheth all things, yea, the deep things of God.' The function of the Holy Spirit is not only to reveal truth as it is in Christ, but also to explore truth. The word 'searcheth' in our text is a most interesting one in the original. Herschel H. Hobbs tells us that 'the term is found in ancient manuscripts for a professional searcher's report, and for the search of customs officials.'[7] Just as an experienced customs official brings to light the hidden articles from a traveller's suitcase, so the Holy Spirit, in a more meaningful sense, explores the deep and hidden things of God and makes them

[6] John 14:26
[7] *The Epistles to the Corinthians* (Grand Rapids: Baker Book House, 1960), p. 23.

understandable and available to the humblest Christian who is prepared to trust this indwelling Revealer and Explorer! The apostle John shares the same secret when he writes his children in the faith: 'Ye have an unction from the Holy One, and ye know all things.'[8]

This amazing phenomenon of spiritual revelation is what baffles the intellectuals of every age. The philosophers and scientists have been able to understand how it is that even unlettered minds can appreciate and discuss truths that are utterly hidden from the world at large. The answer, of course, is that there is such a thing as spiritual illumination. When Peter made that great confession concerning the Deity and Messiahship of Jesus Christ, the Master commended him with these significant words: 'Simon Barjona ... flesh and blood hath not revealed it unto thee, but my Father which is in heaven.'[9]

Do you know anything about this spiritual illumination in your life? There is nothing more wonderful than to share in the revelation and exploration of the Spirit of God. Anyone who has reached this point can say with the apostle Paul: 'Now we have received, not the spirit of the world, but the spirit which is of God; that we might know the things that are freely given to us of God.'

But for the complete comprehension of the Christian message, there must be not only spiritual initiation and illumination, but also *spiritual interpretation*. 'Which things also we speak, not in the

[8] I John 2:20
[9] Matthew 16:17

words which man's wisdom teacheth, but which the Holy Ghost teacheth; comparing spiritual things with spiritual.' Now we reach a point in Paul's argument where we need to follow him very closely. These words which we have just quoted are often used as a proof text by the proponents of verbal inspiration – a doctrine which is both biblical and true. But Paul here says 'we speak,' not 'we write.' Thus he is referring not so much to inspiration as to interpretation. He is teaching us that the knowledge of truth can be arrived at by an understanding of two necessary essentials.

First, the Spirit's use of language – 'Which things also we speak, not in the words which man's wisdom teacheth, but which the Holy Ghost teacheth.' It cannot be emphasised enough that he who knows the mind of God also chooses the words of God to interpret divine truth. This is essentially the ministry of the Holy Spirit. What an importance this places on the Scriptures throughout this church age. His work is to interpret the Bible to men and women who know the experience of spiritual initiation and illumination. Let it be stressed, however, that the Spirit never speaks outside of the context of the divine revelation we call the Holy Bible. That is why we need to give special attention to His use of language. Not one jot or title is inconsequential. Jesus said: 'Heaven and earth shall pass away, but my words shall not pass away.'[10] And He also added: 'When he, the Spirit of truth, is come, he will guide you into all truth.'[11] This

[10] Matthew 24:35
[11] John 16:13

is the secret of interpretation: the Spirit using His own words to make known the mind of God.

But with the Spirit's use of language, there is also the Spirit's terms of reference – 'The Holy Ghost... comparing spiritual things with spiritual.' Now commentators have found it extremely difficult to expound this sentence. Some say it means 'matching spiritual things with spiritual words.' Others maintain that it reads 'interpreting spiritual things to spiritual men.' I am personally convinced that both contentions are right. The point the apostle Paul is making is that 'no prophecy of the Scripture is of any private interpretation.'[12] The Holy Spirit has His terms of reference, and through the body of truth as we know it in the Bible, there is sufficient support for every cardinal doctrine we hold dear.

What is more, we have what is known as a Christian tradition which is made up of the contributions of *spiritual* men down through the centuries. So we are not left to guess about divine revelation. There is no truth which is vital to Christian life and practice which has not the support, both of divine revelation and Christian tradition. When Paul writes to Timothy concerning the comprehension and communication of divine truth, he says: 'And the things that thou hast heard *among many witnesses*, the same commit thou to faithful men, who shall be able to teach others also.'[13]

So Paul concludes this amazing paragraph by pointing out that 'the natural man receiveth not the

[12] II Peter 1:20
[3] II Timothy 2:2

things of the Spirit of God: for they are foolishness unto him: neither can he know them, because they are spiritually discerned.' In other words, without spiritual initiation, illumination and interpretation, divine truth is nothing more than foolishness to the unregenerate – the man of the world. He looks upon revelation as an absurdity. Once we have understood this we have an explanation of the attitude which is adopted by the non-Christian to spiritual things. We must therefore be patient with him and pray that he may submit to the terms of divine revelation.

On the other hand, says the apostle, 'he that is spiritual judgeth all things, yet he himself is judged of no man.' In other words, the man who knows spiritual initiation, illumination and interpretation possesses a faculty which enables him to sift and examine things divinely revealed, as well as things human and natural. At the same time, he cannot be subject to examination and judgement by the one who is destitute of the Spirit. No unregenerate person has the right to criticise or judge a Christian regarding his personal faith in Christ. He is without the faculty of spiritual discernment, and therefore cannot understand the nature of the miracle which has taken place. Just as he cannot judge the Christian, so he cannot instruct the Lord. It is nothing but human ignorance, if not human impertinence for the natural man to raise his voice against the God he is unwilling to accept.

By way of contrast, however, the Christian has the mind of Christ, and this is the transcendent thought with which Paul concludes. The wisdom of God is nothing less than the mind of Christ. The word 'mind' here means 'intellect' or 'consciousness.' We have the consciousness of Christ, the mind of Christ, the outlook of Christ. This is not the same word which Paul uses in the Epistle to the Philippians (Chapter 2). There it is the disposition of Christ; here it is the intelligent understanding, or wisdom, of Christ.

How wonderful it is that you and I, by spiritual initiation, illumination, and interpretation, can know the very mind of the Son of God! And the best of it is that throughout time and eternity we are going to continue to explore that mind of Christ, and so become more and more like Jesus. What a vast universe of knowledge, life and blessing stretches out before us! Even to contemplate it makes us feel like Isaac Newton when he exclaimed: 'I am like a little child standing by the seashore, picking up a pebble here and a pebble there, and admiring them while the great sea rolls in front of me.'

So Paul climaxes a mighty subject with the loftiest of concepts. What he is in fact saying to these Corinthians is that if they know the initiation, illumination and interpretation of the Holy Spirit they will know the mind of Christ. And to know the mind of Christ is to know unity of thought, life and practice. There is no division in the mind of Christ; therefore, there can be no division in the local church that knows the mind of Christ.

We cannot examine what Paul has had to say on this subject of The Comprehension of the Christian Message without concluding that there is an inseparable link between the anointing of the Spirit and the mind of Christ. Only as we know this anointing can we communicate the mind of Christ. We may well ask, therefore, how a person can know this anointing of the Spirit. Surely the answer to that question is to turn to the perfect Example, even that of our blessed Lord. You will remember that His anointing took place on the banks of Jordan. From His mother's womb He was filled with the Holy Spirit, but the anointing came later at His baptism. As we examine the Gospel narrative there appear to be three conditions, or laws, that were fulfilled in order to experience that anointing.

The first was the law of righteousness. Approaching John, Jesus said: 'Suffer it to be so now: for thus it becometh us to fulfil all righteousness.'[14] 'Righteousness' is obedience to the revealed will of God in all areas of life. Without this righteousness no one can know the anointing of the Holy Spirit. The Bible says that God gives the Holy Spirit 'to them that *obey* him.'[15] The reason why Christian people do not know the anointing of the Spirit is because they are not prepared to pay the price of obedience in all matters of faith and practice.

But with the law of righteousness there was the law of yieldedness. We read that 'Jesus... was baptised.'[16] In other words, He handed Himself over to John in an act of utter yieldedness. No one can be baptised without submitting himself completely to the baptiser. And it is equally true that no one can be anointed

[14] Matthew 3:15
[15] Acts 5:32
[16] Matthew 3:16

with the Holy Spirit without self-surrender. This is what Paul means when he says, 'If ye live after the flesh, ye shall die: but if ye through the Spirit do mortify the deeds of the body, ye shall live. For as many as are led by the Spirit of God, they are the sons of God.'[17] Self-effort has to die if the Holy Spirit is to take over in Lordship and leadership in our lives.

Then there is a third law: it is the law of prayerfulness. Luke tells us that as Jesus was 'being baptised, and *praying*, the heaven was opened, and the Holy (Spirit) descended in a bodily shape ... upon him.'[18] Now while the Holy Spirit comes to indwell a believer at conversion, the Scriptures make it clear that the anointing of the Spirit is a subsequent and continuous blessing. In other words, the anointing I knew yesterday is not sufficient for today. There is no fixation point in the experience of spiritual power. So the Lord Jesus said: 'If ye then, being evil, know how to give good gifts unto your children; how much more shall your heavenly Father give the Holy Spirit to them that ask him?'[19] He also told His disciples to 'tarry ... in the city of Jerusalem until (they were) endued with power from on high.'[20] You will remember that it was while they were praying and waiting on the Lord that they experienced the outpouring of Pentecost.

We need to ask and go on asking, if we are to know the anointing of the Spirit. To experience this anointing is to know both the mind and might of Christ in

[17] Romans 8:13–14
[18] Luke 3:21,22
[19] Luke 11:13
[20] Luke 24:49

the comprehension and proclamation of the Christian message. The reason why our witness is so ineffective is because we are not prepared to bow to the laws of righteousness, yieldedness and prayerfulness.

D. L. Moody learned this secret, and even though, to a certain extent, he was untrained and unlettered, he was used like few evangelists in the history of Gospel preaching. Indeed, it is on record that on one occasion a group of ministers were discussing him in connection with a possible crusade in their city. One young man rose to his feet and said, 'Why have we to invite D. L. Moody anyway? Has he a monopoly of the Holy Spirit?' After a pause a discerning man quietly replied, 'While Mr Moody may not have a monopoly of the Holy Spirit, it is very evident that *the Holy Spirit has a monopoly of him.*'

Moody's secret can be yours and mine – *when* we are prepared for the Spirit's monopoly of our lives. Then, and only then, can we know the 'anointing from the Holy One'[1]; then, and only then, can we appreciate and communicate the Christian Message for Contemporary Man.

---

[1] I John 2:20